T0023734

WICKED!

NATIONAL
GEOGRAPHIC
KiDS

DEADLIEST ANiMALS
ON THE PLANET

NATIONAL GEOGRAPHIC
WASHINGTON, D.C.

GREAT WHITE SHARK

Imagine being famous enough to have your own theme song! Enter the great white—and its enormous mouth made up of about 300 razor-sharp teeth. A great white's teeth are lined up in rows, so if the animal loses one, another is ready to take its place. If those chompers aren't enough to make these animals scary, a great white's size and speed should do the trick. They can swim at about 35 miles an hour (56 km/h), can grow up to 20 feet (6 m) long, and can tip the scales at up to 2.5 tons (2.3 t), making them the largest predatory fish on the planet.

Great whites spy-hop: They poke their head out of the water to look for prey.

One great white shark tooth can be more than 6.5 inches (16.5 cm) long.

CORROBOREE FROG

This little critter is pretty—pretty deadly, that is. The brightly colored pattern on this Australian amphibian's skin lets other animals know that it's poisonous. There are many kinds of poisonous frogs, but corroboree frogs stand out from the crowd—their bodies have the ability to make poison. (Other poisonous frogs get their poison from foods that they eat.) The corroboree frog stands out for another reason, too: Unlike many frogs, it walks instead of jumps!

PORCUPINE

Quill you leave me alone? A porcupine's quills normally lie flat against its back. Once threatened, though, this rodent fluffs its sharp spines up and away from its head, neck, and back to let potential predators know that it's not going to be an easy meal. Porcupines can't shoot their quills, but the quills can release when touched, so any animal that tries to take a bite of this prickly prey is going to have a sore mouth ... or worse! Those quills aren't only sharp—they're also barbed on the ends, making them difficult (and painful) to remove.

GIANT HORNET

The size of this insect alone makes it absolutely alarming. Giant hornets have a body that grows to nearly two inches (5 cm) long—that's about five times the size of a honeybee! The preferred prey of giant hornets, like mantises, honeybees, and other kinds of hornets, better watch out! Giant hornets use their mandibles—parts of their mouth used for biting and cutting—to take down their prey. They've been known to wipe out an entire honeybee hive in mere hours!

COOL!

GRAY WOLF

A wolf's piercing howl is enough to send chills up anyone's spine. This call of the wild is one way that a wolf communicates with other members of its group, called a pack. A wolf's pack is extremely important during a hunt. Cooperation allows wolves to bring down prey much larger than them, like moose or elk. Wolves are also seriously smart hunters, and sometimes work together to herd long-legged prey into places where they might lose speed or stumble, like snow-drifts and muddy riverbeds.

TARANTULA

Hairy? Check. Creepy-crawly? Double check. This spider might remind you of a startling Halloween decoration. Earth's biggest tarantula, the goliath bird-eater, has an impressive 11-inch (28-cm)-wide leg span. As its name suggests, this tarantula is big enough to feast on birds, which definitely adds to the fright factor. As scary as they appear, though, tarantulas aren't usually inclined to bite when frightened. Instead, they fling barbed hairs from their bellies at the threat. These hairs irritate would-be predators' eyes or skin, likely driving them away. So, really, most of the hair-raising is done by the tarantula itself.

When threatened, the goliath birdeater makes a hissing sound by rubbing its legs together.

Tarantulas can regrow legs and some of their internal organs.

HAGFISH

Any predator that grabs on to this animal may find itself with a problem to untie. Hagfish have squishy bodies that allow them to tie themselves into a knot. This power is pretty useful—scientists think the hagfish's twisting ability and loose, baggy skin help them slide out of predators' jaws. If that's not enough, hagfish also secrete mucus-like slime—and a lot of it. The slime sticks in the gills of fish that see hagfish as an easy snack, landing the predator in a sticky—and dangerous—situation.

GRIZZLY BEAR

Ever hear the phrase "hungry as a bear"? During the fall, grizzly bears eat almost constantly in an effort to gain enough fat for winter. Although they are especially fond of salmon, and will prey on land animals like elk and deer, grizzlies aren't strictly meat-eaters. As omnivores, they'll munch on berries, nuts, and other plant parts. Grizzlies dig for roots and other buried food using the massive hump of muscle between their shoulders and their up to four-inch (10-cm)-long claws to tear through soil.

CASSOWARY

Meet one of the world's deadliest birds. The cassowary, which is native to Australia, is flightless, but it packs a powerful kick. Its middle toe is armed with a single sharp claw that can be up to five inches (13 cm) long and is able to slice open any animal that tries to pick a fight. The bird's warrior-like appearance is also aided by the casque, a helmet-shaped structure on top of its head. The casque might be helpful in attracting mates, or in turning up the volume on the bird's loud, booming calls.

WHOA!

TASMANIAN DEVIL

This marsupial has a nasty temper! When disturbed, Tasmanian devils growl, scream, lunge, and bare their teeth. In addition to a famously fierce disposition, a Tasmanian devil has an oversize head that includes some of the world's most powerful jaws. The animal's strong bite gives it the power to eat almost anything—and it will. A Tasmanian devil chews on and devours whatever it can find, including animal bones and household trash.

THREE DEEP DWELLERS

Earth's oceans are vast and deep—really deep. On average, the ocean floor is a little more than two miles (3.2 km) below the water's surface, but some parts are close to seven miles (11 km) deep. Let's dive in to meet three creatures that live in the darkest parts of the ocean.

ATLANTIC WOLFFISH

Wolffish have some pretty impressive teeth. The ones that line the animal's upper jaw grab and hold prey, while a second set in the animal's throat crush its meal as it swallows.

GOBLIN SHARK

Goblin sharks have jaws that are able to move forward and backward. Once the sharks spot a fish, they drift close to it, barely moving. Then they quickly shoot out their jaws, grabbing their prey.

What's my next catch of the day?

ANGLERFISH

If looks alone don't convince you that this fish is deadly, consider this: Female anglerfish dangle a glowing, fleshy lure in front of their mouth to attract prey. When curious fish get too close ... SNAP!

A golden dart frog's only predator is a small snake that is unharmed by the frog's poison.

The frog got its name because people put the frog's poison on darts for hunting.

GOLDEN DART FROG

This picture shows what might be the world's deadliest frog. A wild poison dart frog's body is only about the size of a large paper clip, but it has enough poison to kill almost any animal in the Colombian rainforest it calls home. Its skin serves double duty: It's the site of the glands that contain the animal's poison, and the brightness of the frog's skin warns other animals to stay away. Though this little critter's poison is very deadly, it might turn out to be very useful. Scientists are studying ways to use one of the chemicals in dart frog poison as medicine to help relieve pain.

ANACONDA

When it comes to snakes, the green anaconda is a real heavyweight—literally. Earth's heaviest snake, it weighs up to 550 pounds (250 kg). These big reptiles lack venom; they instead hunt by waiting in water for prey. When an animal bends to take a drink, the anaconda grabs it, wraps around it, and squeezes. Although these snakes are known to swallow large prey like deer and crocodiles, they tend to stick to smaller meals, like other reptiles and fish.

WOW!

HOUSE CAT

Beneath the fur of this *awww*-worthy animal beats the heart of a fierce hunter. Like their wild cousins, house cats are natural and fearsome predators, nabbing their prey about once out of every three tries. Their instinct to chase anything that moves is apparent to anyone who's seen them take on a catnip mouse. If you have a pet cat, keeping it indoors as much as possible doesn't only help keep your cat safe—it also helps keep local wildlife like birds from becoming house cat prey.

STINGRAY

A predator that grabs this animal by its tail is probably in for a nasty surprise. Stingrays have a sting, or spiny barb, located somewhere along their whiplike tails. The sting easily cuts through skin, allowing the ray's venom to enter its attacker's body. Stingrays aren't aggressive, and they generally glide away from a fight. Most people who do get stung don't see the ray on the ocean floor and accidentally step on it!

SOLENODON

Poor eyesight doesn't stop the solenodon from finding its next meal. This shrewlike mammal has an extra-special sniffer. As it walks through the forests of Cuba, Haiti, and the Dominican Republic, it uses a long, flexible snout to sniff the ground for insects and worms. It also can take on larger prey like amphibians and reptiles, disabling them with a venomous bite. Solenodons are best left alone, because they tend to go from zero to full-on freak-out with little to no warning.

No two
African wild dogs'
coats are exactly
the same.

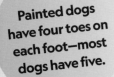
Painted dogs have four toes on each foot—most dogs have five.

AFRICAN WILD DOG

You can call these animals African wild dogs or African painted dogs—just make sure you also call them super-skilled hunters. These animals hunt in packs of seven to 15 members in territories scattered over the African continent. Working together, the dogs can run after and bring down speedy prey like antelope and wildebeests. Their success rate is one of the best on Earth: About nine of every 10 hunts results in a meal. The dogs aren't only fast sprinters—they're also distance runners, chasing after prey for almost an hour. These persistent predators are also great at sharing; each member of the pack, including pups, gets some of the meal.

IGUANA

This reptile has a message for predators: Get off my tail! If an iguana feels like it's losing ground in a fight, it will thrash its tail from side to side. And if the animal's tail is grabbed, the tail can safely break off, giving the iguana time to make a getaway. This escape artist's tail isn't the only thing these animals use to fight: Their mouths are full of serrated (saw-edged) teeth!

They might look like underwater plants, but *Palythoa* are animals. Relatives of corals and anemones, *Palythoa* release a nasty toxin. The poison has a purpose in the wild. It acts a little like a force field and kills or prevents other corals and sponges from growing too close to the *Palythoa*. This superior survival skill means the *Palythoa* has few natural predators.

BUMBLEBEE

This bee looks as furry and soft as a stuffie. But bumblebees can, and will, sting—especially when they think their nest is under attack. A bumblebee's sting doesn't carry as much venom as other members of the bee family, so stings are generally less painful. Every fall, the whole bee colony dies off, leaving only the dominant female, called the queen. The queen hibernates underground in the winter and rebuilds a new colony in the spring.

EUROPEAN MOLE

European moles are big trouble ... if you happen to be an earthworm. The European mole lives mostly underground, using a keen sense of hearing to find its prey. It's almost always looking for food and will eat more than half its body weight daily. Although the mole has been known to eat insects and even small animals like mice, its favorite food is earthworms. The mole's saliva has a substance that stops the earthworm in its tracks, making the wiggly prey easier for the mole to eat!

AWE-SOME!

MEERKAT

Meerkats are a watchful bunch—one animal always stands guard while other family members hunt.

What are *you* looking at? Groups of meerkats, called gangs or mobs, are forces to be reckoned with. These small mammals tirelessly work together to defend their burrow from attackers, and they are often able to drive off dangerous predators, including venomous animals like scorpions and snakes. Rival mobs will also face off with one another, battling with claws and teeth to claim territory. It's a matter of survival. In the African grasslands and deserts, food and water can be difficult to find. Mother meerkats are especially fierce fighters and will do what it takes to make sure that their pups (babies) have plenty to eat and a safe place to live.

Female meerkats will often take care of another meerkat's pups while she's out hunting.

HARPY EAGLE

Everything about this bird is supersize! Harpy eagles have a wingspan of about six feet (2 m), and legs about as thick as a young child's wrist. Those legs end in claws, called talons, that curve more than five inches (13 cm) away from the bird's toes. The harpy eagle uses its talons to grab and crush unsuspecting prey like monkeys, sloths, iguanas, and even wild deer in the rainforests of Mexico, Central America, and South America.

Hedgehogs are prickly little characters, thanks to the 5,000 or so spines that cover their bodies. When attacked, they hiss and curl up into a ball, protecting their soft stomach and leaving the predator with a mouthful of spines. As if that's not unappetizing enough, hedgehogs also deliberately make themselves smell and taste bad by participating in a behavior called "anting." They chew on strong-smelling substances and then lick themselves, spreading foamy spit over their bodies. Ew!

PREY POWER!

CUTE BUT DEADLY

Don't mess with these cuties! These animals might look cute enough to cuddle, but don't even think about it. They hide some harmful surprises beneath their sweet appearances.

TIGER QUOLL

A tiger quoll's personality matches that of the big cat whose name it shares. These little marsupials are fierce predators—they often catch prey bigger than themselves. They also growl and hiss when they're upset.

WHITE-TAILED DEER

This little cutie might be spreading some big trouble. The skin of white-tailed deer is often home to ticks that carry Lyme disease, which can make animals and people sick.

TICK

This Stalk doesn't stand a chance.

GIANT PANDA

Pandas' jaw muscles help shape their adorable round faces. These muscles are strong enough to shred the tough bamboo that makes up most of a panda's diet—and to help the animals defend themselves.

SEA CUCUMBER

Curious-looking relatives of sea stars, most sea cucumbers can be found scooting along slowly near the bottom of the ocean. Although these animals' soft bodies might seem to make them easy targets for hungry fish, sea cucumbers have a spectacular defense against would-be predators: They are able to push some of their organs out of their bodies. In many kinds of sea cucumbers, the organs are coated in toxic mucus—a double delivery that's definitely enough to drive most animals away.

COW

It may be hard to believe, but more people are hurt by cows than by sharks every year. Or maybe it's not so hard to believe. An average full-grown cow can weigh about 1,500 pounds (680 kg). Some breeds of cattle have big horns and aren't shy about using them when frightened or to defend their territory. When a heavy animal with big horns charges, there's the scary possibility of more than a little damage.

COYOTE

For some animals, less is more. Unlike many other members of the dog family, coyotes don't hunt in large packs, preferring instead to pursue prey with either a partner or a small group. Cooperation pays off: Teamwork can help a pair of coyotes hunt some tough prey. For example, a porcupine can become a meal if one animal flips the rodent over while the other goes after its soft belly. Coyotes also occasionally buddy up with badgers, working together to dig up and capture animals that live underground.

PLATYPUS

The duck-like bill and webbed feet of the platypus might make it seem harmless. But male platypuses have a special weapon: small, sharp barbs called spurs right above their back feet. Most of the time, they use these spurs against one another when they compete for mates. If attacked, though, the platypus can drive its spurs into the threat. And there's more: Platypus spurs can release venom that injures or even temporarily paralyzes other animals.

The dragon's sense of smell can detect prey more than a mile (1.6 km) away!

KOMODO DRAGON

This dragon doesn't breathe fire, but it's still dangerous! Komodo dragons are the world's largest lizards, measuring up to 10 feet (3 m) long and tipping the scales at more than 300 pounds (136 kg). But their size isn't the only thing that makes them fierce. These reptiles also have a keen sense of taste, using their tongue to sample the air to detect prey. They will wait patiently along paths deer and other animals commonly use, then spring out when one passes by. A single bite laced with venomous saliva is usually enough to bring down a dragon's meal.

A Komodo dragon egg is about the size of a grapefruit.

CANE TOAD

It's the toad that ate Australia! Well ... sort of. In 1935, a few thousand cane toads were brought from South America to Australia. Their job: to help keep down the number of beetles eating sugarcane. But the toads didn't eat many beetles. They did eat just about everything else, including a lot of local wildlife. To make matters worse, Australia has only a few predators that are able to eat the invasive, toxic amphibian. The result? Hundreds of millions of cane toads hop around Australia today.

That's a big baby with its mouth open for food! Its mother, a female cuckoo, wouldn't win any parent of the year awards. She lays her eggs in another bird's nest, then flies away, letting the other mother bird hatch and raise her chicks. The baby cuckoo isn't innocent, either—it pushes the other eggs and chicks out of the nest, then keeps its large beak open, gobbling up all the food meant for the other bird's chicks.

WICKED!

LANCEHEAD

This snake is a master spy! Lanceheads are pit vipers—snakes that use organs called pits to sense an animal's body heat. The pits, found between the eyes and nostrils, help lanceheads figure out both the location and size of a nearby animal so they can decide if the animal is a predator or prey. If it's a bird or lizard, the lancehead will strike, using its powerful venom to bring down its meal.

PRAYING MANTIS

Nope, it's not something out of a science fiction movie! A praying mantis may look a bit like an alien, but it's actually one of the best predators on Earth. Big eyes give the mantis extremely good vision, allowing it to see in 3D, like humans can. It can also turn its head in a half circle, so very little escapes this insect's attention. When a mantis spots a possible meal, it sneaks up on it slowly, then grabs and traps it with its spiky forelegs.

45

AFRICAN BUFFALO

Each family, or clan, of buffalo has a pathfinder—an animal that leads the clan to food.

With a nickname like "the black death," it's no surprise that animals should steer clear of this creature. An African buffalo's mood can go from sunny to stormy in the blink of an eye. If it does, it's best to find somewhere else to be: These animals will mob predators and are strong enough to toss a lion in the air! Although these buffalo aren't territorial, they're well equipped to defend themselves and their herd. Both male and female buffalo have two giant curved horns that almost meet in the center. In males, they form a hard, bony shelf called a "boss," a word that definitely describes the African buffalo!

Members of a herd will doze off with their heads resting on one another.

RED-TAILED HAWK

These birds of prey can often be spotted perched on light poles or other high places, keeping a sharp eye out for rabbits, squirrels, snakes, and other small animals. These hawks are daring acrobats in the air, swooping, diving, and sometimes even passing prey to one another during flight. Their screeching cry can send shivers up anyone's spine. It's so chilling that it's sometimes used as a TV or movie sound effect for the cry of a bigger bird of prey, like an eagle.

When you hear the name wolverine, you might think of claws and some superhero-size healing powers. Although this amphibian doesn't have true claws, it does have a pretty sharp way of defending itself. When attacked, the frog breaks its own toes, forcing the sharp bones through the skin. If the attacking animal is scratched or cut, it might drop the wolverine frog in surprise, giving the frog time to get away and find a place to hide and rest until its toes are repaired.

PREY POWER!

49

GIANT AFRICAN LAND SNAIL

There's more to this snail than its incredible size. Although originally from East Africa, it's able to survive anywhere warm. That's bad news for farmers and gardeners: It's not a picky eater and will munch its way through vegetable gardens and crop fields. These mollusks also pick up some extra nutrition by chewing on nonliving things like stone and concrete, leaving behind a trail of mucus-like slime.

AWE-SOME!

SALTWATER CROCODILE

Saltwater crocodiles are the world's largest reptiles—males can grow to about 17 feet (5 m) long and weigh well over a ton (0.9 t). The saltwater croc eats just about anything it wants, including water buffalo and deer. Crocs lurk in shallow water, patiently waiting before bursting through the surface with a huge push of their powerful tails. They often drag their prey beneath the water and hold it there until it drowns, then tear it apart and swallow it in chunks.

POISONOUS OR VENOMOUS?

It's nearly impossible to discuss deadly animals without using the words "venomous" and "poisonous." Here's how to detect the difference between the two.

VENOMOUS animals use a body part, such as their teeth or a stinger, to deliver their poison. Just touching a venomous animal won't cause harm—it has to bite or sting.

POISONOUS animals have something toxic (poisonous) in their bodies. They're harmful if touched or eaten.

RHABDOPHIS

POISONOUS

BRUNO'S CASQUE-HEADED FROG

VENOMOUS

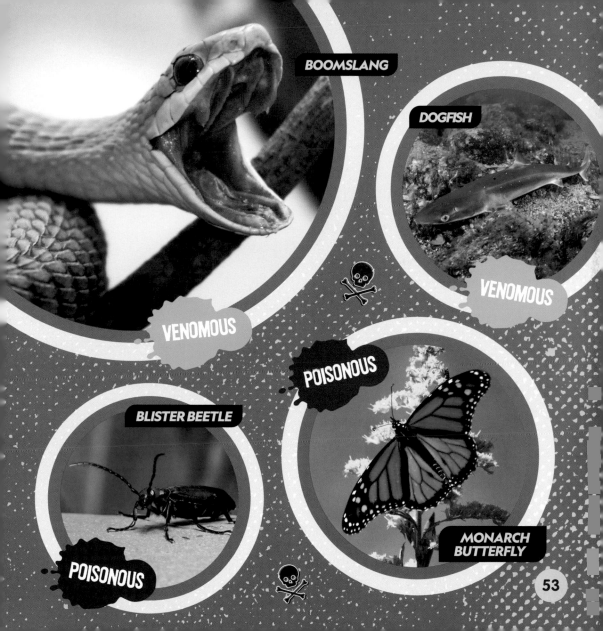

BOOMSLANG

DOGFISH

VENOMOUS

VENOMOUS

POISONOUS

BLISTER BEETLE

MONARCH BUTTERFLY

POISONOUS

53

HONEY BADGER

With a name so sweet, who could guess that this animal can drive away large, fierce creatures like African buffalo and lions? But a honey badger does, counting on its claws and skin for protection. Its skin is so thick that most insect stingers and snake fangs can't get through it. It also hangs somewhat loosely from the honey badger's body. If the honey badger is caught, it can twist and turn so that the other animal often loses its grip.

FRILLED SHARK

The frilly gills that give this shark its name don't do much to disguise its terrifying appearance. Frilled sharks live in some of the deepest parts of the ocean, and they can top six feet (1.8 m) in length. Each of the 60 or so teeth in the frilled shark's mouth has five points. The tip of each point faces the back of the animal's mouth, hooking squid and other prey so the shark can swallow them whole.

JAGUAR

The name of South America's largest cat comes from an Indigenous word that means "animal that kills in a single bound." Indeed, this cat is one of the world's greatest hunters, with jaws strong enough to crush a turtle's shell. The jaguar isn't only deadly on land—it's also a threat to fish, small crocodiles, and other aquatic prey. Jaguars don't mind the water and will go for a swim when they're hot—or when they're hungry.

BLACK MAMBA

If an animal sees the dark-colored inside of this snake's mouth, it's lights-out! This snake's skin can be brown, gray, or olive, but it is named for the black-blue inside of its mouth, which is only visible when the snake is threatened or about to strike. This reptile won't attack unless bothered, but when it does strike, the result can be deadly. Its venom is some of the most toxic stuff on Earth. Just two drops can kill a human if the victim doesn't receive antivenom.

WHOA!

Portuguese man-of-wars got their name because they look like 18th-century Portuguese battleships.

PORTUGUESE MAN-OF-WAR

Groups of more than 1,000 Portuguese man-of-wars have been spotted floating on the ocean's surface.

This animal may look like a jellyfish, but it's not. It's not even one animal—it's many! Portuguese man-of-wars are made of four individual animals called polyps. Together, they add up to trouble as they float along the surface of the Atlantic, Pacific, and Indian Oceans. Inside some of the Portuguese man-of-war's long, colorful tentacles are small barbs that are launched like tiny harpoons at prey. Once the barb's venom stuns the target, the man-of-war drags its prey to its mouth. These animals don't attack people, but they do sometimes drift into unsuspecting swimmers. Their venom is so strong that even tentacles of dead man-of-wars can still sting.

ZEBRA

You'd better back up! Zebras use their powerful kick to defend themselves against lions and other ferocious African savanna predators. Male zebras also will raise a hoof (or two) to kick other zebras that try to steal their food or move in on their territory. They'll even use their teeth to grab a threat and throw it to the ground. Zebras have notorious tempers and are always ready to defend themselves when necessary.

SHOCKING PINK DRAGON MILLIPEDE

The shocking pink dragon millipede lives on the leafy floor of the woods in places like Thailand and China. If its spiky appearance doesn't immediately turn off predators, its color does. That brilliant hue is a signal that the insect's body is loaded with a deadly poison. The millipede even smells like poison, making it possibly one of the least appetizing meals anywhere on Earth.

ASSASSIN BUG

This group of insects has a killer name! About 7,000 related insects are called assassin bugs, and they all share a few of the same characteristics—like a stabbing mouthpart that they use to pierce prey before slurping up their meal. But assassin bugs display a dazzling range of differences, too. Some lie in wait for prey before pouncing, while others sport a large, jagged plate of armor. One even carries some of its victims around on its back—a move that probably helps these beastly bugs hide from predators.

BABOON

That's not a yawn—it's a threat. To send a warning to predators, baboons show off their pointed canine teeth, which can be well over an inch (2.5 cm) long. Baboons don't hesitate to flash their teeth in their group, or troop, either. Those powerful chompers are also visible when a baboon screams. Each troop helps crown their top male and female by having yelling contests. The animals that yell the loudest and longest usually end up dominating the group.

BENGAL TIGER

There are big cats, and then there are bigger cats. Bengal tigers are some of the most massive cats on Earth—they can weigh up to 500 pounds (227 kg). This fierce predator lurks in the grasslands and forests of India, searching for big animals like wild pigs, deer, and buffalo. Tigers use their excellent night vision to hunt after the sun sets, stalking prey for 20 minutes or more before pouncing. As carnivores, tigers eat only meat—and they eat a lot of it! A single tiger usually eats about 25 pounds (11 kg) in a day but can gobble 60 pounds (27 kg) or more in a single meal.

Tigers' stripe patterns are like human fingerprints: No two are the same.

Unlike many other cats, tigers are good swimmers, thanks to their partially webbed toes.

65

COTTONMOUTH

This is one tricky, venomous reptile! When threatened, an adult cottonmouth coils its long body and opens its mouth wide, showing the cottony white skin inside to startle predators. As a pit viper, the snake has facial "pits" between its eyes and nostrils. These special organs allow the cottonmouth to sense infrared heat that comes from warm-blooded prey. That means the snake can always detect prey ... even in total darkness.

TARANTULA HAWK

This wasp's sting is said to be one of the most painful in existence. Good news, though—tarantula hawks tend to avoid humans. The news for tarantula spiders, though, isn't as bright. A female wasp will use its powerful sting to kill a tarantula. Then it seals the dead spider inside the spider's den with one of the wasp's own eggs. When the egg hatches, the young wasp uses the tarantula for food until it's big enough to dig out of the den.

DEADLY APPETITES

What kind of animal is the world's deadliest? Well, that depends on how you define the word "deadly." Meet three animals that have some pretty big appetites, chowing down on huge amounts of prey in a single meal.

BROWN BAT

Imagine eating a meal that weighs more than you do! Brown bat mothers can eat more than their body weight in insects every night, including mosquitoes and other insects that are human pests.

BLUE WHALE

A blue whale's diet is mostly krill, tiny shrimplike animals that are only a few inches long. Blue whales eat around 40 million of these animals every day—a total of about 8,000 pounds (3,600 kg)!

Slurpie, anyone?

GIANT ANTEATER

A giant anteater's tongue is more than two feet (0.6 m) long and coated in sticky spit. The anteater feeds by pushing this long tongue into ant colonies. Once the ants are stuck on the tongue, the anteater slurps them up. A single giant anteater can gobble up to 30,000 ants and termites every day.

ADÉLIE PENGUIN

What Adélie penguins lack in size, they make up in attitude. Although they're only about 2.3 feet (0.7 m) tall, they're not afraid to drive off predators like seals with a swift smack of a flipper. They're just as bold in their search for prey—and any animal caught by an Adélie stays caught. The inside of the penguin's beak is covered with hooks that point toward the bird's throat and prevent fish from wriggling away.

PREY POWER!

CHIMPANZEE

Prey be wary—this is one smart predator! Chimps are closely related to humans, so it's no surprise that they solve problems in some of the same ways that we do. For example, they make tools to help them get food, like using blades of grass to fish for ants, and using sticks as spears to hunt small animals. Chimps can be humanlike in other ways, too. They're not always good at sharing, whether it be territory, food, or mates.

BROWN RECLUSE

Other spiders might be bigger and flashier—but no spider has venom as damaging to people as the brown recluse's. These spiders live in the south-central United States, and they lurk both outdoors in woodpiles and under rocks and indoors in dark attic and basement corners. The brown recluse is only about the size of a U.S. quarter, and its fangs aren't long enough to puncture through clothing. Though the little animals are shy and only bite people when they feel threatened, their bite can cause skin damage.

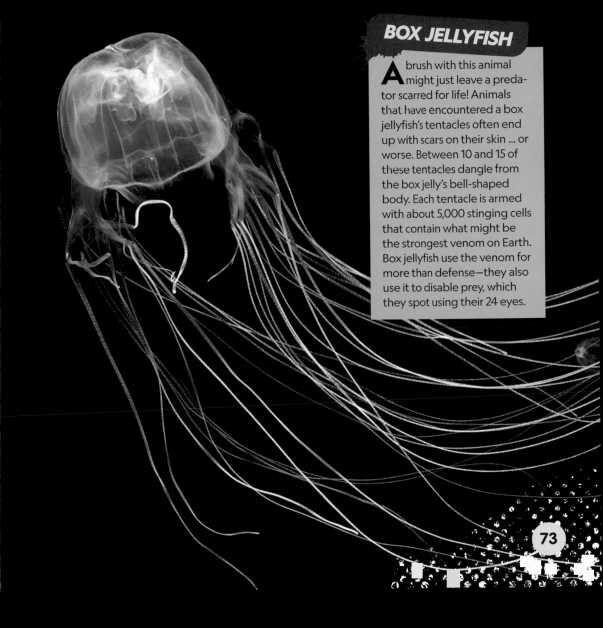

BOX JELLYFISH

A brush with this animal might just leave a predator scarred for life! Animals that have encountered a box jellyfish's tentacles often end up with scars on their skin ... or worse. Between 10 and 15 of these tentacles dangle from the box jelly's bell-shaped body. Each tentacle is armed with about 5,000 stinging cells that contain what might be the strongest venom on Earth. Box jellyfish use the venom for more than defense—they also use it to disable prey, which they spot using their 24 eyes.

Lorises are the only primates known to make venom.

SLOW LORIS

This primate takes a slow but deadly approach to life among the leaves. Lorises move at a snail's pace through the trees of Southeast Asia, with three of their limbs always clinging tightly to a branch. They would be ideal targets for birds of prey, except for one thing: Lorises have patches along their inner arms, right by their elbows, that make venom. When threatened, a loris clasps its hands on its head and hisses, swaying back and forth like a snake. If this display isn't enough to scare off predators, the loris quickly licks the venom from its arms, then gives whatever's bothering it a nasty toxic bite.

Lorises' large eyes help them see as they look for food at night.

NORTH AMERICAN RATTLESNAKE

Buzzzzzz. Rattlesnakes make this sound by rapidly vibrating their tails, causing the hollow scales at their tips to clatter against one another. It's a clear warning to North American predators and people alike to back off. The snakes grow more rattles on their tails as they get older, and rattles are replaced as they break or fall off. This noisy shake should make you move, or you're risking a bite from venom-filled fangs!

OMG!

JAGUARUNDI

You're not likely to spot this incredible animal! Jaguarundi aren't often seen in the wild. They're super shy around humans and very skillful at avoiding being caught on camera. Because of their short legs and rounded ears, they're sometimes nicknamed "weasel cats." Unlike many other cats, jaguarundi are diurnal—active during the day. They hunt for small animals like rodents and armadillos during early morning and near sunset, and often head to a watering hole for a drink in the afternoon.

SPERM WHALE

Sperm whales are able to dive to some killer depths. These big mammals spend most of their lives well beneath the ocean's surface. Able to hold their breath for over an hour, they dive down more than 3,280 feet (1,000 m) in search of food. Sperm whales work together to hunt—some members of the group herd prey like squid into a small area for the rest to snatch up and gobble down. Those meals are supersize—sperm whales swallow well over a ton (0.9 t) of food every day!

BULLET ANT

If there were a "world's most painful sting" competition, the bullet ant would win a top prize. One of Earth's smallest creatures, this ant is found in South American rainforests. Although bullet ants don't usually attack people, they do use their venom to defend their nests from predators like monkeys. And an animal bitten won't likely forget it—the effects of this insect's venom are about 30 times the strength of a honeybee sting and can last up to an entire day.

ORCA

Orcas are sometimes called killer whales, but they're actually the largest members of the dolphin family. The "killer" part of that name, though, is accurate. Orcas prey on just about anything smaller than themselves, including seals, dolphins, and great white sharks. The body part that makes them one of the most efficient predators in the sea, though? Their brain. Orcas are seriously smart and often work together with other members of their pod, or group, to track down and trap their next meal. One of their favorite moves is to use their tails to create a wave that crashes over the shore, pulling any animals dozing on the beach into the water.

Orcas have a mouthful of three-inch (7.6-cm)-long, razor-sharp teeth.

These fast, super-sleek animals can cut through the water at 33 miles an hour (53 km/h)!

BLUE-RINGED OCTOPUS

Beauty or beast? Only about the size of a golf ball, the blue-ringed octopus is far from being one of the biggest octopuses in the Pacific Ocean. But it is one of the deadliest. When alarmed, this shy little creature develops a pattern of brilliant blue circles on its body—a warning that it's venomous and best left alone. The octopus usually uses its paralyzing venom to kill prey like small fish, crabs, and shrimp.

BEAVER

Busy as a beaver? More like bad-tempered as a beaver! Beavers are highly territorial and won't hesitate to go after an animal that wanders too close. Their long incisors, or front teeth, are orange because they contain iron. These chompers are super strong, able to not only bite through wood, but also into anything that threatens the beavers' kits, or babies. That said, beavers' construction talent does most of the work of keeping them safe—many animals won't swim across pools of water that form behind a beaver dam.

83

LEOPARD

This predator may look like it's lounging on a limb, but it isn't ready for a catnap. Leopards sit in trees to keep an eye on the world below. When these big cats see prey, they pounce from on high. A male leopard is strong enough to haul a small giraffe into a tree. Once its prey is safely stashed there, the leopard can eat in peace without worrying about losing its hard-earned meal to lions and other predators.

PREY POWER!

HORNED LIZARD

This animal's defense is bloody disgusting! When threatened, the horned lizard inflates its body to make its spiky scales stand out. If that doesn't work, it breaks some of the blood vessels around its eyes and squirts a jet of blood up to three feet (1 m) away. To top it off, the reptile's blood contains a substance that makes it smell and taste really, really bad to common threats, like dogs, cats, and coyotes.

TOP CHOMPS

Which animal has the most powerful bite? Each has its own strong points. Some animals bite down on a small area, while others grind over a large one. Many experts agree that the saltwater crocodile has the strongest bite—but here are some other contenders.

DRIVER ANT

Driver ants use the two gripping parts around their mouth, called mandibles, to tear into their prey, which includes not only other insects, but also animals much larger than themselves, like rats.

GROUND FINCH

The ground finch may seem pretty harmless, but its bite is nothing to mess around with! If this bird were the same size as a *Tyrannosaurus rex,* it would win the bite-strength battle ... hands, er, wings down!

BULL SHARK

Great white sharks might be the most famous sharks, but bull sharks have a bigger bite. They use that force to grab marine prey, including dolphins and sea turtles.

Now who's the Shark Star?

CHEETAH

Want to talk about speed? Cheetahs are the world's fastest land animals, able to race up to 70 miles an hour (113 km/h) over short distances. That sprinting power is possible thanks to cheetahs' amazing body parts. Unlike most cats, cheetahs' claws are always partially extended, giving them super grip on the ground. Their backbones are also extra flexible, allowing the cats to stretch their bodies to cover about 30 feet (9 m) of ground in one bound. Those are some swift cats!

GILA MONSTER

People used to think that this lizard's breath was pure poison. Its breath is safe, but the Gila monster's bite is venomous. This reptile prefers to try to scare predators away by hissing, but if it decides to bite, it goes all in. The Gila monster bites down and gets a grip on its attacker, chewing on the other animal to force its venom deep into the bite. It's nasty, but it usually works, with the predator dropping the Gila monster and giving the reptile time to flee.

AFRICAN CRESTED RAT

These furry rats have a deadly secret. African crested rats chew on the bark of a poisonous tree, then lick a special strip of fur on their sides. Like magic, this strip soaks up the poison. When threatened by a predator, the rat freezes in place, then puffs out this strip of hair, positioning its body so that the predator will get a mouthful of poison-soaked fur. If the predator survives, it will definitely remember to leave the next rat it sees alone!

SEA OTTER

Do sea otters have cute faces? Yes. Are they playful? Absolutely. Should they be considered cuddly? No! Swimmers, kayakers, and dogs that wake a dozing sea otter find out pretty quickly that a mouth strong enough to chomp through the shells of sea urchins, crabs, and snails is also strong enough to leave behind a painful bite! These clever predators store tools like rocks in folds of their armpits, and they use them to bash open their prey. This special skill comes in handy because sea otters eat 25 percent of their body weight in food every single day!

These beetles spray in a series of short bursts—up to 500 bursts in one second!

BOMBARDIER BEETLE

Biting and stinging insects have absolutely nothing on the bombardier beetle. When startled, the beetle releases a spray of bad-tasting chemicals from its abdomen. In case that doesn't sound bad enough, consider this: The spray is the temperature of boiling water. Bombardier beetles can control the direction of this spray and have killer aim, sending the mixture toward an attacker's eyes and face. And the spray isn't one and done—the beetle can keep firing away, so there's no time for the predator to regroup and try to attack a second time. Bombs away!

Bombardier beetles live on every continent except Antarctica.

DALMATIAN PELICAN

Though their name might suggest otherwise, these birds don't have spots. One of the heaviest freshwater birds, Dalmatian pelicans can weigh about 30 pounds (13.6 kg) and have wings that stretch more than 11 feet (3.3 m) from tip to tip. They have a huge appetite, gulping down as much as four pounds (1.8 kg) of fish every day. It's a group effort to get full: The pelicans work together to chase fish into shallow water before scooping them up into their large bills.

SEA LION

Sea lions aren't afraid of a fight! When challenged, these animals attack back, thrashing and biting to escape from predators, or slamming their necks into another sea lion to defend their territory. If a sea lion loses ground to an orca or another aquatic predator, it can launch itself out of the water at high speed and escape the threat. And when the sea lion is the hunter itself, prey like fish, squid, and octopuses better watch out! A sea lion can quickly dart through the water at about 25 miles an hour (40 km/h) to snag a snack.

WOW!

TIGER SHARK

With their stealthy hunting skills and super appetite, tiger sharks really live up to their name. Though other sharks tend to take a taste of something before deciding if it would make a good meal, these fish don't. Tiger sharks eat anything, including trash like old tires that unfortunately fall into the ocean. Tiger sharks swim very slowly, trying not to attract attention as they hunt for prey. When they spot a potential meal, they put on a burst of speed, catching and swallowing their meal whole.

Most amphibians aren't venomous—they don't bite or sting to deliver poison. The Iberian ribbed newt, which lives in Spain, Portugal, and parts of Morocco, is an exception. When caught, it sticks its ribs through the sides of its body. The ribs poke a hole in the predator's mouth, allowing the newt to drive venom deep into the hole, much like a painful bee sting. Ouch!

GIRAFFE

It's hard to imagine a giraffe, with gentle eyes and slow, graceful movements, on the attack. But attack they can—and do. Male giraffes, called bulls, fight over mates using a motion called necking. During these battles, giraffes use their head and neck to smack each other's bodies. The loser of these battles ends up with more than just hurt pride. Sometimes they can have cuts and bruises from their opponent's ossicones—hornlike structures on the top of their head. When facing a predator, giraffes rely on their long legs. They have a kick strong enough to stun an attacking lion.

Giraffes aren't silent—they groan, growl, hum, and bleat.

Because of their large size, giraffes have only a few predators, including crocodiles and lions.

ELECTRIC EEL

Here's a shocking fact: The amount of electric current generated by a large electric eel would be enough to knock down a horse. These fish can generate a charge to escape the jaws of predators like crocodiles or to stun small fish to eat. They also have another use for all that current. Because they can't see very well, eels emit a small pulse of electricity like radar to help them find their way while swimming through muddy water.

NORTHERN SHRIKE

This bird is small but mighty. Northern shrikes keep a sharp eye out for prey while perched on posts and treetops. When they spot smaller birds or mice, they dart after them, killing their prey with the hooked end of their beak. Because northern shrikes also don't like to waste food, they will sometimes put captured prey on a spike such as a twig or thorn if they're not hungry, saving it for later.

WILD BOAR

These aren't your everyday barnyard pigs. Wild boars are strong, aggressive animals that live in a huge range of habitats. These animals are as comfortable in a swamp as they are in a forest. They're not picky about their diet, either, and will eat everything from roots and berries to worms and fish. They can weigh over 200 pounds (91 kg) and can run at speeds of about 25 miles an hour (40 km/h). Although these animals are a favorite food of bears, big cats, and other large predators, they can cause a lot of damage by charging and goring would-be predators with their sharp tusks.

PREY POWER!

Scientists may not officially agree on which of Earth's snakes is most deadly—but the inland taipan is one of the top candidates. Need a reason why? Here are three: The snake bites quickly, its strikes are right on target, and its venom is the most powerful on the planet. In fact, the venom from a single bite of an inland taipan can kill 100 people! But don't worry too much—antivenom is available, and this reptile prefers to save its venom for its favorite meal, the long-haired rat.

GROSS DEFENSES

From claws to teeth to venom, all animals have some way to defend themselves. Some animals have methods that are a little (or a lot) grosser than most.

TURKEY VULTURE

A turkey vulture may vomit on a predator that gets too close. Given that these bald-headed birds like to eat dead animals, that's a stomach-turning defense.

POTATO BEETLE

Beetles tend to be pretty easy prey for birds. But the potato beetle coats its back with its own poop, which hardens into a shield that looks, smells, and probably tastes terrible.

Stinky? Stylish is more like it.

HOOPOE

The brightly feathered hoopoe bird coats its eggs with goo that smells like rotten meat, then does the same to its own feathers. The stink likely drives away predators while killing germs that might harm the eggs.

AMERICAN ALLIGATOR

If you're looking at a lake, river, or swamp in the southeastern United States, you're looking at a possible home for the top predators in the neighborhood. American alligators will hang out anywhere they can find a meal, including local ponds and golf courses. When a gator clamps onto its prey, it will do what's called a "death roll." This violent spinning maneuver not only disorients prey but also helps break it into pieces.

PRAIRIE DOG

Prairie dogs may look cute and harmless, but beneath that fuzzy coat hides the heart of a fighter. These little animals are fast and fearless when cornered, using their claws and teeth to drive off predators like ferrets. One kind of prairie dog will even tackle an animal that attempts to invade its territory. The white-tailed prairie dog kills off ground squirrels that might want to move into their neighborhood.

PREY POWER!

COOL!

LIONFISH

This fish certainly looks like it's king of the reef! Red lionfish live along coral reefs in the warm waters of the Pacific and Indian Oceans. The fish's "mane" is actually made of venomous spines used to defend itself. Like an undercover spy, it relies on speed and camouflage to capture larger prey, but it has a different plan when it comes across a school of small fish. It uses its fins to sneakily herd them into a corner, and then chows down.

Rhinoceroses are some seriously big animals. The biggest species of rhino, the white rhino, can tip the scales at 5,000 pounds (2,268 kg), and has horns that grow to be about two feet (0.6 m) long. Although few animals are big or brave enough to take on an adult rhino, these massive mammals still use their bulk and that horn to defend themselves and their territory. They also have notoriously bad eyesight: When startled, they can charge at full speed into objects like rocks and trees.

Peregrines often build their nests on skyscraper ledges.

The name "peregrine" comes from a Latin word that means "wanderer."

PEREGRINE FALCON

You'll need sharp sight if you want to catch this animal in action! Soaring through the sky at dizzying heights, peregrine falcons dive headfirst at speeds reaching about 200 miles an hour (322 km/h) to knock prey from the air in a flurry of feathers. As a champion of the sky, a peregrine enjoys a diet of mostly other birds. Some, like gulls and geese, are much larger than the falcon itself. The peregrine doesn't tend to miss its targets, large or small. It takes aim at its prey by using its amazing eyesight, some of the best of any animal.

AMERICAN BADGER

With short, strong limbs, and claws well over an inch (2.5 cm) long, the American badger is a digging machine, and underground prey like rats, gophers, and mice had better beware. Badgers know a lot about being underground themselves, as they build and use multiple dens for everything from sleeping to storing food. A badger will fiercely guard its den's opening, backing into the entrance so that its sharp teeth and sharper claws are all that's visible.

With their enormous pincers, or claws, these animals look like something right out of a scary movie! Coconut crabs live on islands scattered in the Indian and Pacific Oceans. These big land crabs weigh up to about nine pounds (4 kg) and can be three feet (1 m) long from leg to leg. Coconut crabs eat dead animals, fruit, seeds, and, of course, coconuts. When the colossal crabs use their claws, they can exert a massive force of 740 pounds (3,300 newtons)!

WHOA!

BARRED OWL

This owl isn't only a greedy predator that eats just about any kind of small animal—it's also a terrible neighbor! These birds don't build nests, choosing instead to take over nests built by other animals. So, it's the neighborhood watch to the rescue. Smaller birds like woodpeckers and crows often band together and "mob" the owl, swarming all around it to try to chase it away.

MONGOOSE

A lot of animals are fierce hunters, but few have what it takes to go after cobras! Mongooses can tolerate snake venom and often hunt venomous snakes, as well as prey like rats and insects. Mongooses have the distinction of being deadly in another way, too. They've been used to try to control rat populations in places like Hawaii and the West Indies. Unfortunately, they did the job a bit too well and have caused a big drop in the number of not only rats but also birds and other animals.

MANTIS SHRIMP

This tiny critter packs a punch that is one of the strongest, and speediest, in the world. The colorful mantis shrimp is found in warm ocean waters, but it might feel more at home in a boxing ring. When within range of a crab or other tasty animal, it wallops the prey with one of its clublike front claws. Although the shrimp isn't especially big, only about four inches (10 cm) long, it can punch hard enough to break glass. Like any good boxer, it also uses these skills to defend itself. When a predator approaches, the crafty crustacean backs up into its burrow and gives any animal that approaches a good whack.

Mantis shrimp don't do well in aquariums because they eat almost anything.

Because of this animal's bright colors, it's often called the peacock mantis shrimp.

HYENA

Hyenas' loud "laughter," a noise they make to call other hyenas to a food find, isn't funny. These carnivores are serious hunters. Although they have a reputation as scavengers that live on lions' leftovers, hyenas actually find and kill most of their own food. And once they do, the feast is short—a group of hyenas can gobble up a 500-pound (227-kg) zebra in less than half an hour, with each hyena easily stuffing away more than 30 pounds (14 kg) of meat.

BLACK-FOOTED CAT

This little kitty is the deadliest cat on Earth. (No, really.) Black-footed cats weigh much less than the average house cat, but these compact creatures are able to catch about a dozen birds and rodents in a single night. This makes these cats the most successful hunters of all their cousins—a big cat like a lion might take several months to catch the same number of prey. Black-footed cats prowl the grasslands and deserts of Africa, startling their prey out of tall plants before capturing it with a speedy pounce.

SNOW LEOPARD

The elusive snow leopard silently stalks through high Asian mountain ranges. Its coat helps the cat blend in unseen as it searches for prey like ibex and mountain sheep. These big cats can eat quite a bit, since it takes a lot of energy to hike up and down the cold, rocky cliffs where they live. Snow leopards are well-equipped for life in the mountains, though. These cats not only use their three-foot (1-m)-long tail to keep their balance, but they also use it as a blanket, wrapping themselves up in it to stay warm.

AWE-SOME!

PITOHUI

When talking about birds, the word "poisonous" doesn't usually come up. Thanks to the pitohui, perhaps it should. Pitohui are striking birds, with deep red eyes and black and orange feathers. Those feathers carry a powerful poison—and scientists aren't quite sure why. The most likely reason is that the birds' bodies get the poison from a beetle they eat, and it acts like a natural insect repellent to keep lice and other harmful pests away.

DEADLY MYTHS— BUSTED

Sometimes it can be a bit hard to tell where the truth about an animal ends and the tall tales begin. Here are a few stories that just happen to be false.

DADDY LONGLEGS

THE MYTH
Daddy longlegs spiders are extremely venomous, but can't bite because they have very small mouths.

THE FACT
These spiders can and do bite people— but there's no evidence that their venom is strong.

THE FACT
A vulture's great sense of smell helps it sniff out dead animals to eat, but it can't look at a healthy animal and know that it will soon be on the menu.

THE MYTH
Vultures know when an animal is going to die.

VULTURE

THE MYTH
Earwigs crawl into people's ears to lay their eggs.

THE FACT
These insects don't bother people at all, unless handled.

EARWIG

REEF STONEFISH

Can you see the fish hidden in this picture? The reef stonefish is a master of disguise. Its skin color and texture help it look almost exactly like a piece of coral reef. A line of exceptionally venomous spines on its back protects the fish from other fish that are sharp enough to spot it. This solitary fish digs itself into a shallow pit near a reef and spends its days perfectly still—until a fish swims over it. Then, like a vacuum on turbo speed, the stonefish sucks its meal into its large mouth.

WICKED!

BLACK WIDOW

Does the red hourglass on this female black widow mean that your time is running out? The distinctive markings on this arachnid's shiny black abdomen have helped give it a fearsome reputation. Like many spiders, however, the black widow is shy and usually bites people only when afraid or threatened. Male black widows have every reason to be afraid of females, though. Females often eat the males after they've mated!

GORILLA

Gorillas are Earth's largest apes, weighing up to 400 pounds (181 kg) and growing to about 5.5 feet (1.7 m) tall. They live in groups called troops, led by a large male called a silverback. Gorillas are mostly gentle giants—but look out if another male tries to challenge a silverback's leadership. The troop's leader will scream, beat his chest with cupped hands, and charge at his rival. If the scare tactics fail to work, the two will fight, with the winner taking charge.

CUTTLEFISH

This animal is an underwater master of disguise. Cuttlefish, which are related to octopuses and squid, are able to change the color and shape of their bodies to seamlessly blend into rocks and coral reefs. This camouflage makes them almost invisible to both predators and prey. Some cunning cuttlefish change color rapidly as they approach a crab or a fish, distracting it so that the cuttlefish can move close enough to grab its meal.

Any animal in lion territory is potential prey, but lions usually eat zebras and antelope.

LION

Meet the queens of the African savanna! African lions are some of the most famous predators on the planet—and they live up to their fierce reputation. Adult lions have nothing to fear except other adult lions. Females, called lionesses, are faster than males and do most of the hunting. Lionesses hunt in groups, usually at night. They crouch low in the grass, getting as close to prey as possible before pouncing. Should the prey manage to make a getaway, the lighter, quicker lions chase it toward the stronger lionesses—and the chase ends with a leap and a snap of jaws.

Male lions defend their pride's territory by driving away intruders.

FULMAR

The name "fulmar" means "foul gull," and this bird definitely has a disgusting defense! Both adult and baby fulmars defend themselves by throwing up an oily fluid all over potential predators. The stuff smells absolutely terrible—like rotten fish—and is really hard to remove. That's bad for furry predators, but much worse for feathered ones. The oily stuff can act like glue, sticking feathers together and making it difficult, if not impossible, to fly.

BRAZILIAN WANDERING SPIDER

These spiders can be found wandering across the floors of South American rainforests at night, searching for mice, insects, and other spiders to eat. This spider's size—its legs can span six inches (15 cm)—is likely enough to make your skin crawl. If not, then maybe this will: Some scientists think it's the world's most venomous spider. Brazilian wandering spiders are also called "armed" spiders, because they raise their front legs into the air and wave them back and forth when threatened. Talk about a wicked warning signal!

POLAR BEAR

Polar bears are not only the largest Arctic land predators, they're also some of the most dangerous. These animals have a strong sense of smell and follow their noses to find holes in the ice that seals and other animals use to breathe. A bear will wait next to a hole until a seal pops up to take a breath; the bear then reaches through to quickly grab its prey with one swipe of a paw.

PIRANHA

Small fish, big bite! Piranhas swim in large groups called shoals through the freshwater rivers and lakes of South America. Not only are their mouths lined with saw-edged teeth, they can also bite with great force. But much of this fish's deadly reputation is based on myths. Although a shoal of piranhas can eat large prey like capybara, they're not likely to attack a healthy one. And some kinds of piranhas don't eat meat at all—they live on seeds and other plant parts.

Spitting cobras aim for the threat's eyes—and hit them nearly every single time.

SPITTING COBRA

Cobras also spray their venom to keep large animals from accidentally stepping on them.

Get back! When threatened, spitting cobras squeeze venom through small holes in their fangs. The result? A spray that can shoot more than six feet (1.8 m) from the snake's body. To make the effect even more terrifying, spitting cobras will hiss and lunge while spraying. Although the venom can't get through most animals' skin, it can be extremely harmful to eyes, even causing blindness. Spitting cobras, which live in Africa and Asia, only spit to drive away possible predators like mongooses and secretary birds. When hunting for prey like rodents and birds, they release their venom through a bite, like most cobras do.

KANGAROO

Young male kangaroos often box, or "spar," using their arms to push and hit each other. Sparring might look pretty dangerous, but young 'roos rarely get hurt. The strongest fighters will someday use their sparring skills to become the leader of a group of kangaroos, called a mob. If a kangaroo is in danger, though, it doesn't use its arms, instead using its much bigger and stronger back feet to deliver a crushing blow.

WOW!

COUGAR

Cougars, also called mountain lions, pumas, or panthers, stalk South America and western North America for deer, coyotes, and other prey. Cougars often spring from rocky ledges onto their prey, killing it with a big bite to the neck. The cougar, although large in size, is not grouped with big cats like lions and tigers. All big cats can roar, and cougars can't. They can purr, though—a bit of an unexpected noise from such a deadly hunter!

BIG-HORNED SHEEP

R eady, set, charge! Male sheep, also called rams, use their famous curled horns to fight with other males for mates and for the right to lead the herd. The two animals lower their horns and charge at each other over and over again, sometimes at speeds of 20 miles an hour (32 km/h). It must be an exhausting fight—those big horns weigh about 30 pounds (13.6 kg), more than all the bones in the ram's body combined.

Slow-moving, small ... and extremely deadly. Found in warm ocean waters from East Africa to Hawaii, the textile cone snail feeds on small animals as part of its diet. Like other snails, the textile cone snail drills a hole in its prey's shell with a body part called a radula, then releases a liquid that digests the animal's body. But unlike other snails, the textile cone snail uses extremely toxic venom, some of the most harmful stuff on Earth.

IT'S ALL IN THE (DEADLY) DETAILS

Sharp claws; big teeth; long, thrashing tails—the owners of the most dangerous body parts in the animal kingdom might surprise you. Check out these three animals and their unusual deadly details.

GIANT ARMADILLO

A giant armadillo's large claw is nearly eight inches (20 cm) long, close to a quarter of its body length. That would be like a six-foot (1.8-m) person having a 1.5-foot (0.5-m)-long fingernail!

THRESHER SHARK

A thresher shark's tail, which makes up more than half its body length, is a dangerous weapon. The shark rushes into a school of fish, whipping its tail at lightning speed. Any fish unlucky enough to be struck by the shark's tail is likely to become dinner.

All this fuss over two teeth?

MUSK DEER

Is this a deer or a vampire? The male musk deer's "fangs," which average about four inches (10 cm) in length, are likely used to fight with other deer.

GOLDEN EAGLE

When it comes to catching prey, this raptor does not follow the one-size-fits-all approach: A golden eagle's plan of attack depends on its target. On one hunt, a golden eagle might soar high in the sky above a flying bird and then crash down on it, slamming it out of the sky. On its next pursuit, the eagle will fly much lower, slowly and quietly, to grip its talons on ground prey like rabbits. These brilliant hunters also aren't shy about attacking animals much larger than themselves, including small deer and even young brown bears.

This shark streaks through the ocean, using its wide head to survey the seafloor for prey. The hammerhead shark's rectangular head and wide-set eyes make it an extremely efficient hunter. These sharks stick close to the ocean floor, home to their favorite food: rays. After the shark spots one, it uses its big head to pin the ray to the ground. These fish aren't aggressive toward humans, though, and tend to swim away rather than attack.

COOL!

CANADA GOOSE

What happens when you mix a large, short-tempered bird with a whole lot of humans? Nothing good. Canada geese build their nests on the ground near bodies of water—including the ones found on golf courses and in parks. Male geese defend their nest, and they take that task seriously. Any animal or person that gets too close will likely get a pinch from the bird's beak or a whack from its wing. Want to avoid unpleasant encounters like these? Give the birds their space.

MOSQUITO

Mosquitoes are more than just annoying insects. They're the world's deadliest animals. Their bite doesn't have venom, but it can sometimes spread diseases like malaria. Mosquitoes can pick up malaria when they bite a person who has the disease, then pass it on to the next person they bite. Malaria is very uncommon in the United States, but it affects many other parts of the world. Fortunately, it can be treated with medicine.

This fox's brown fur changes to white in the winter, making it harder for predators to spot in the snow.

Arctic foxes have thick fur coats—even on their feet. This helps muffle their footsteps as they approach prey.

146

ARCTIC FOX

These cute little kits will grow up to be terrors of the cold and icy Arctic. Prey can be difficult to find in Earth's northernmost spot, so these animals eat anything they can track down, including dead animals and other animals' droppings. Arctic foxes use their supersharp hearing to find their favorite prey: small rodents called lemmings that tunnel underground. When foxes tune in to the scurrying below the snow, they use their big paws to dig down and snatch a meal.

WHOA!

BEARDED DRAGON

Bearded dragons are not shy about showing their feelings if another dragon tries to move into their territory. The lizards' "beard," which covers their neck and chest, is made of pointed scales. When these lizards are upset, their scales stick out and turn black, telling other lizards that they'd better move on. Angry bearded dragons will also puff up their bodies, trying to look as big as possible. If the outsider doesn't take the hint, the lizards will lunge, delivering a painful bite.

AFRICAN ELEPHANT

An African elephant's size is generally enough to keep predators away—but it never hurts to have a backup plan. Male elephants have large tusks they can use to scare off lions or hyenas. An equally important weapon for this mostly gentle giant is its famous trunk. An elephant's trunk has thousands of muscles and is strong enough to lift more than 700 pounds (318 kg), as well as to deal a pretty nasty blow to any animal that comes too close.

149

BUDGETT'S FROG

This amphibian has a big mouth from day one. Most tadpoles nibble plants with tiny teeth. But Budgett's frog tadpoles have special jaws that help them swallow their prey—which includes other tadpoles—whole. Adult frogs are aggressive, lunging forward to feed on insects, tadpoles, and smaller frogs. They use their big mouth for defense, too, shrieking and lunging with their mouth open at anything they think is a threat.

BLUE GLAUCUS SEA SLUG

The delicate-looking blue glaucus sea slug, sometimes called the blue angel or the blue dragon, is anything but angelic. It feeds on one of the ocean's most venomous creatures, the Portuguese man-of-war. The blue glaucus is able to take the stinging barbs from the man-of-war's tentacles and move them to the ends of its feathery body. Then, if attacked by a fish or other predator, the blue angel can use the barbs for its own defense.

151

DRAGONFLY

You're looking at an insect with a serious appetite. A single dragonfly can catch and eat hundreds of insects every day. Dragonflies' hunting success is due not only to their huge eyes, but also to their double wings, which allow them to hover in one spot, like helicopters. These intelligent insects can also outsmart their meals. During a chase, dragonflies are able to guess what path their prey is going to try to use as an escape route. But no need to worry—dragonflies are harmless to humans. What looks like a long stinger is actually a body part that the female dragonfly uses to lay eggs.

Dragonflies catch about nine out of every 10 insects they chase.

Young dragonflies, called nymphs, live in water, preying on worms, insects, and even small fish.

153

WARTHOG

Warthogs are far from the only animals that have tusks—but they are some of the only ones that have them for the purpose of defense. Warthogs have two pairs of these overgrown teeth, both of which curve away from the animal's mouth. The upper ones are longer, but the lower ones are razor-sharp. Warthogs use these to fight with other members of their group, called a sounder, or to drive off larger animals that think these piglike creatures would make a good meal.

SEA URCHIN

Almost every part of this animal seems to be doing double duty. A sea urchin's spines aren't just for protection. Because the animal can move each spine, it uses them to snag prey or, if the urchin ends up on its back, to walk! Sea urchins usually move with rows of tubelike feet. They also use these feet to scale rocks and to grab food. An urchin's amazing feet even help the animal breathe and act as eyes to help it see!

BIRD-DROPPING SPIDER

When it comes to outmaneuvering predators, sometimes gross is the way to go! The bird-dropping spider's markings and body shape make it look a lot like bird poop. The spider sits almost motionless during the day, with its legs pulled in close to its body. But at night, the hunt begins. Hanging down from its web by a thread of silk, the spider releases a scent that attracts male moths to its web, then grabs them from the air when they get too close.

SCORPION

From its pinching claws to the tip of its stinging tail, the emperor scorpion, one of the largest of the more than 2,000 kinds of scorpions in the world, can grow to eight inches (20 cm) long. These arachnids use both ends of their body to hunt, crushing smaller prey like insects, or stinging larger animals like lizards. Scorpions vomit digestive juices from their stomachs onto their prey, then wait for it to turn to liquid before slurping it down.

TOXIC SMELLS

These animals don't pass anyone's smell test. Meet three of nature's stinkiest critters.

STINKBUG

These insects create a stink in more ways than one. When startled, stinkbugs release a foul-smelling mix of chemicals. They also damage crops and invade homes and other buildings in large numbers.

HOATZIN

The hoatzin, a bird that lives in the rainforests of South America, is said to smell like a barnyard! That's due to its diet. The hoatzin's body makes and passes lots of smelly gas as it digests the leaves it eats.

SKUNK

Skunks aren't afraid to use their teeth and claws in a fight—but they're known for their smelly spray. Skunks aim their spray toward another animal's face, temporarily blinding it so the skunk can escape.

Paws up ... FIRE!

159

YELLOW JACKET

Successful predators—bad tempers. Yellow jackets are small stinging wasps, not bees, found throughout North America. Unlike most honeybees, some yellow jackets will chase after an animal (or person), especially one that has disturbed their nest. Yellow jackets are important predators of many smaller insects, including grubs that cause damage to gardens and farms. They also like drinking sweet liquids—so keep those out of sight if you want to enjoy your picnic!

SAILFISH

With a huge dorsal fin on their backs and a long, swordlike bill, sailfish are real forces of nature, leaping at amazing heights out of the water when trying to escape predators. They're smart, too—sailfish work together to catch a meal. They use their large fins to herd schools of sardines or other fish into a small area. Once they have the school surrounded, they slash their bills quickly back and forth, stunning some of the fish so that they are easy to catch.

FISHER

Although some people call them fisher cats, these animals aren't cats at all. They are excellent hunters and exceptional climbers, though. Members of the weasel family, fishers have hairy feet and claws that are always at least partially extended, both of which help keep them from slipping as they climb. Their ankles can also turn halfway around, allowing fishers to come down from trees face-first instead of tail-first—never losing sight of their prey.

AWE-SOME!

MOOSE

Keep away from a moose on the loose! The moose's famous antlers, sported only by male members of the herd, can grow to be almost six feet (1.8 m) across. If an animal like a wolf or a mountain lion tries to take down a moose, the moose will defend itself with those antlers and kick with both its front and hind legs. Moose also defend themselves from illness in an unexpected way—by drooling. Moose spit contains a substance that helps kill harmful organisms on the grasses these animals eat.

A pufferfish has four teeth that together form a mouthpart that looks like a beak.

Pufferfish range in size from one inch (2.5 cm) to two feet (0.6 m) long.

PUFFERFISH

Talk about impressive armor! Pufferfish are not graceful swimmers, moving slowly along as they search for food like shrimp and plants to eat. These animals aren't easy targets, though, and make up for their poor swimming skills with a spectacular defense. Pufferfish fill their stomachs with water, blowing up their bodies like balloons when threatened. Some kinds of pufferfish have spines that stick out in all directions when their bodies are inflated, making the animals almost impossible to bite and even harder to swallow. Many pufferfish have one more surprise for animals brave enough to try, though—their bodies are full of poison.

AFRICAN GIANT SWALLOWTAIL

Even a really hungry animal wouldn't be able to stomach the African giant swallowtail. The largest butterfly in Africa, this insect has a wingspan of up to 9.8 inches (25 cm). It's also extremely poisonous. Scientists aren't sure why, but they think it's because the caterpillars munch on the leaves of a toxic plant. Much about these butterflies is a mystery. Female butterflies live and feed in treetops but are rarely, if ever, seen.

RACCOON

Who's that behind the mask? Known for the rings on their tails and their Batman-like "eyewear," raccoons can be found almost anywhere in North America, including in cities and towns. These cute critters don't mind digging through trash to find dinner, a habit that can lead to some aggressive run-ins with pets and people. When startled, raccoons may make a huffing noise, growl, squeal, and charge at the threat.

CHILL

DOLPHIN

Dolphins may look like they're smiling, but inside that cute beak are sharp teeth. Dolphins use them to grab prey before gulping it down whole. Those teeth are also used in fights with other dolphins—older dolphins' bodies usually sport many scars. Dolphins' most deadly body part, though, might just be their clever brains. The mammals have been spotted stirring up mud and using the cloudy water to trick fish into swimming right into their open jaws.

GREAT HORNED OWL

Whooo is fierce enough to take on falcons and other birds of prey? The great horned owl. This large bird has a huge appetite and eats just about anything it can catch, including other owls. It usually hunts at night, swooping down to snatch prey from the ground with its talons. These strong claws squeeze hard enough to kill most prey, and the owl can retreat to a tree or other perch to eat its meal.

69

VAMPIRE BAT

A vampire bat's diet is a liquid one—this little mammal takes flight every night in search of cattle and other large animals from which to drink. It lands next to its sleeping victim and scuttles toward it. Special sensors on its upper lip and nose help it find a spot where blood is flowing close to the skin's surface. Then it uses its supersharp teeth to make a small cut and starts lapping up the blood with its tongue.

Vampire bats will spit up swallowed blood to share with other hungry bats.

These bats are gentle bloodsuckers. They can feast on their prey for more than 30 minutes without it waking up.

171

HORNET MOTH

This insect has a secret: It looks deadly, but it's not. The hornet moth looks a lot like an insect that can deliver a nasty sting. It takes the act even further, mimicking a hornet's buzzing sound. The combination of these imitations is usually enough to make predators decide to get their meals elsewhere. Hornet moths aren't completely harmless, though. The larvae of these insects bore into trees, which damages and in some cases kills the tree.

HORSE

This animal may be domesticated, but it definitely has a wild side. If a horse is cornered, or if a mare is protecting her foal, it will use its whole body to defend itself and members of the herd. A horse can rear up on its hind legs, striking at a threat with its hard hooves, or, if the threat is coming from behind, shoot both hind legs out at up to 50 miles an hour (80 km/h).

WHOA!

LEOPARD SEAL

The ferocity of this animal is more than skin deep! Leopard seals aren't just named for their spotted coats—they also have fierce personalities and expert hunting skills. Some seals are content to dine on fish and other cold-blooded animals, but not leopard seals. These mammals spend much of their day swimming along the edges of Antarctic ice floes looking for penguins, then springing out of the water and grabbing any bird that wanders too close.

DINGO

Packs of these reddish wild dogs roam throughout the continent of Australia. When it comes to hunting, anything goes—dingoes will hunt alone or in small packs. They're especially fond of chasing other famous Australian residents—kangaroos. A pack of dingoes can take down the much larger animal by chasing a kangaroo until it is too tired to fight. Dingoes don't need to fight off any predators, but farmers and ranchers do end up hunting them when the animals make livestock like cattle and sheep fair game.

175

(NOT SO) DEADLY FAKERS

Some of the world's animals are deadly. Others are just good at faking it. Some harmless animals mimic, or copy, animals that are dangerous. Predators that can't spot the difference leave both animals alone—a win-win.

CORAL SNAKE

KING SNAKE OR CORAL SNAKE?

At first glance, king snakes and coral snakes look like they have identical rings of black, yellow, and red. But their patterns are different, as are the snakes. Coral snakes are venomous; king snakes are not.

Let's rhyme: Red touches black, venom lack.

KING SNAKE

BUMBLEBEE OR ROBBER FLY?

Bumblebees have a stinger, but robber flies don't. Robber flies are often mistaken for bumblebees by other animals and humans!

BUMBLEBEE

ROBBER FLY

GRASS MOTH

GRASS MOTH OR TIGER MOTH?

TIGER MOTH

Tiger moths leave a bad taste in a predator's mouth, thanks to their poisonous bodies. Grass moths aren't poisonous at all, but some look enough like tiger moths that birds don't bother them.

177

PECCARY

For peccaries, dedicatedly defending their turf means never going solo. These pig-like mammals live and move in large groups, called herds, that may have more than 50 animals. Although peccaries don't usually attack other animals, they are extremely protective of their territory, both from other peccaries and other animals. A group of them will rush after and drive off even large predators like jaguars, which usually flee rather than risk being trampled.

OMG!

JAPANESE SPIDER CRAB

These animals have seen some things—Japanese spider crabs can live about 100 years. They spend much of that time alone, scuttling solo across the ocean floor looking for dead animals to eat. Their large bodies and long, gangly legs can span a whopping 13 feet (4 m). Their size is enough to keep most animals away, but they do occasionally lose limbs when defending themselves. That's no problem, though—spider crabs can regrow them over time.

GREAT BLUE HERON

Great blue herons hunt by day or night, stealing their way through the tall plants that border wetlands and other bodies of water. Herons will stand still for hours at a time, searching for fish or other small animals to eat. When they spot a meal, they use lightning-fast reflexes to extend their long necks, nabbing prey with a daggerlike beak and then swallowing it whole.

TAMANDUA

The tamandua is one animal that can really make a stink. When frightened, these anteaters can spray liquid that, according to many people, smells worse than a skunk's odor. If the stench doesn't sway an attacker, a tamandua rears up on its back legs, using its thick tail as a third limb for support. This frees up its sharp claws to slash away at any animal that gets too close.

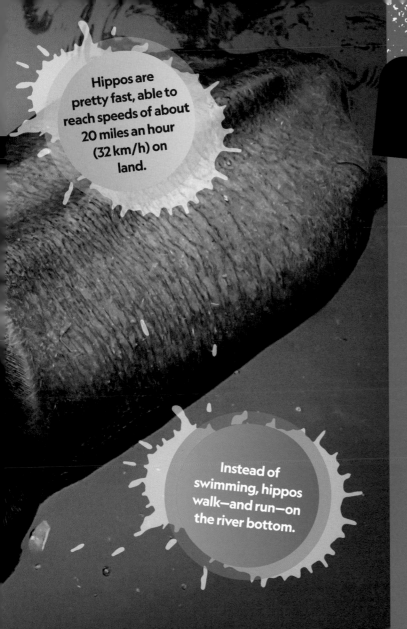

Hippos are pretty fast, able to reach speeds of about 20 miles an hour (32 km/h) on land.

Instead of swimming, hippos walk—and run—on the river bottom.

HIPPO

These large animals look friendly and are plant-eaters, so surely they can't be dangerous, right? Wrong. As the third largest land mammal, hippos can weigh two tons (1.8 t). Male hippos are especially aggressive and will occasionally use their large bodies to charge at boats in their river territory. Hippos also have 20-inch (0.5-m)-long teeth and aren't afraid to use them, especially against anything they think is a threat. These animals spend most of their time in the water but do come out to enjoy the sun. Their skin even makes a greasy substance that acts as a sunscreen. The substance is red, which gave rise to the myth that hippos could sweat blood.

FIRE ANT

Yow! A fire ant's venom causes a stinging, burning sensation. Two kinds of these biting insects live in parts of the southern United States. These ants cause a lot of pain, and not only of the physical kind. Fire ants also destroy crops like corn and wheat, causing people who grow them to lose money. They like to build their nests in homes and garages, and because they need only about a month to grow from an egg to an adult, they can be hard to get rid of.

WOLVERINE

This animal's not a superhero, but it is a super predator! Wolverines are the largest members of the weasel family, weighing a pretty hefty 35 pounds (16 kg). Although they'll nibble on berries and nuts when available, wolverines are mostly meat-eaters—dedicated ones. They will travel up to 15 miles (24 km) to scout for prey like rats, mice, and rabbits. If they can't find any fresh meat, they'll eat dead animals.

DHOLE

This animal is fearless! Related to wolves, foxes, and other members of the dog family, dholes (pronounced "doles") hunt and defend themselves in packs and are courageous enough to drive away tigers. Not bad for small animals—dholes weigh only about 30 pounds (14 kg) but will run, jump, and even swim after a possible meal. Unlike other members of the dog family, dholes don't howl or bark. They use a unique whistling sound to communicate with one another as they hunt for prey.

WICKED!

LAMPREY

This fish is the stuff of nightmares. Sea lampreys latch on to other fish, using their mouths lined with rows of sharp teeth to hang on tightly. The lamprey then feeds on blood and liquids in the host fish. A sea lamprey is an extremely efficient predator, able to kill about 40 pounds (18 kg) of fish every year—that's a lot for a small fish! Unlike most aquatic animals, sea lampreys are able to live in both salt water and fresh water, making them threats to many different kinds of fish.

OSTRICH

An ostrich egg weighs an average of three pounds (1.4 kg).

These flightless birds have a reputation for hiding their heads in the sand when they're threatened. That is a myth—ostriches fight back! The big birds can use their long legs to deliver a crushing kick when they're under attack. Each of the ostrich's legs ends in a foot tipped with two sharp claws, making an ostrich's leg a weapon deadly enough to kill a lion. But ostriches prefer to use their strong legs to run away from danger. Taking strides that are 10 to 16 feet (3–5 m) long, they can sprint short distances at speeds of about 40 miles an hour (64 km/h).

A newly hatched ostrich is only about the size of a chicken.

SNAKEHEAD

Despite its name, this animal doesn't have fangs or venom. This fish does have the ability to do something that most others can't—survive on damp land for the better part of a day. It can live in almost any pond, lake, or river. It can also survive in more polluted water than many other kinds of fish. Once snakeheads move into an area, they tend to take over, hogging most of the food that other kinds of fish need to survive. When food runs low, snakeheads can hop out and wriggle to a new home.

WATER MONITOR LIZARD

Sharp claws, toxic venom, and deadly speed in one animal—that's a water monitor. Found in Thailand and other countries in Asia, these large reptiles will eat anything they can catch, including birds, rats, young crocodiles, and turtles. They are skilled hunters, using their strong legs to dash after anything that moves. They're also common sights in city parks, where they look for food in ponds and lakes.

COOL!

PYTHON

This snake's a record-breaker! Pythons consistently take the title of world's longest snake, measuring up to 30 feet (9 m) long. Like boa constrictors and anacondas, pythons lack venom, and instead use their teeth to grab and hold prey, coil their bodies around it, and squeeze. These reptiles can stretch their jaws over a meal that's five times as wide as their head! It's worth the effort, because the python might not need to eat again for about 10 days.

FLANNEL MOTH CATERPILLAR

Don't cozy up with this caterpillar! Although the larvae of the flannel moth look soft to the touch, they are also one of the most venomous caterpillars in the United States. All that fuzz covers a series of spines that deliver a painful sting. The caterpillars lose their spines after complete metamorphosis turns them into adult moths, but they don't lose all their hair. The adult moth's fuzzy body makes it a tough meal for birds to swallow.

Elephant seals rarely go on land. They leave the ocean only to molt, or shed their fur, and to reproduce.

Male elephant seals can be more than 20 feet (6 m) long and weigh up to 8,800 pounds (4,000 kg).

ELEPHANT SEAL

Male elephant seals use their big, inflatable noses to turn up the volume during mating season, making deafening roars that can be heard from several miles away. That big beak also hides a pair of huge front teeth that are strong enough to break bone. Although these animals don't appear to be particularly graceful on land, watch out in the water. Elephant seals can easily swim at speeds that top 10 miles an hour (16 km/h). They're also champions at holding their breath underwater, able to do so for about two hours while diving beneath the ocean's surface to chase sharks and other prey.

BARRACUDA

Barracuda have a fearsome look, with long snakelike bodies and large eyes. But are they really to be feared? For other fish—definitely. Swimming at speeds of up to 36 miles an hour (58 km/h), barracudas' streamlined bodies can cut through water quickly when they spot prey. The fish grab their prey with not one but two rows of razor-sharp teeth—the teeth in the inner row are long and used to pierce, and those in the outer row are short and used to tear.

WHOA!

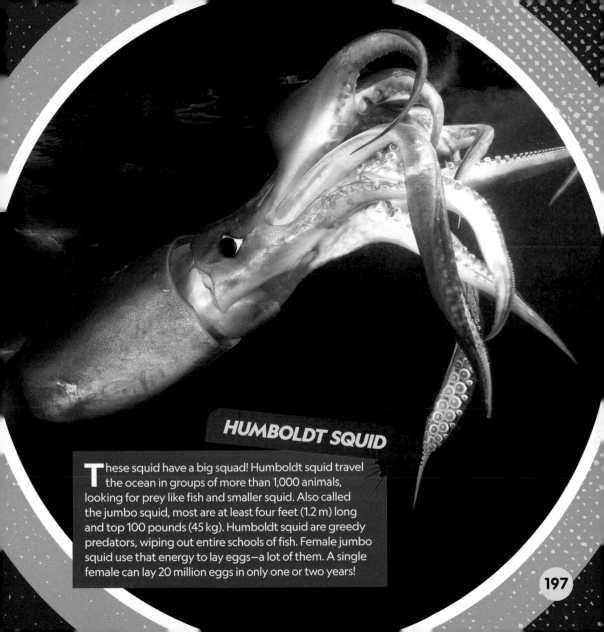

HUMBOLDT SQUID

These squid have a big squad! Humboldt squid travel the ocean in groups of more than 1,000 animals, looking for prey like fish and smaller squid. Also called the jumbo squid, most are at least four feet (1.2 m) long and top 100 pounds (45 kg). Humboldt squid are greedy predators, wiping out entire schools of fish. Female jumbo squid use that energy to lay eggs—a lot of them. A single female can lay 20 million eggs in only one or two years!

BLACK CAIMAN

Black caimans are part of a ferocious family! Related to crocodiles and alligators, these animals feed on fish, reptiles, and large mammals such as the capybara, the world's largest rodent. Like other members of their family, caimans use their teeth to grab their prey and then swallow it whole. No predator is willing to take on these large reptiles, which can grow to be about 15 feet (4.5 m) long—except for humans, who hunt them for their hides and meat.

CROWNED EAGLE

This bird of prey looks like it should be forest royalty! The chicks grow their crown of feathers at about two months of age and start hunting on their own about a year after their flight feathers come in. Crowned eagles are able to kill animals that weigh well over 40 pounds (18 kg), including monkeys and small antelope. These birds are skilled hunters in the sky as well, chasing airborne prey at speeds approaching 100 miles an hour (161 km/h).

WILDEBEEST

What's gnu? Wildebeests, also called gnu, are the largest kind of antelope. Found only in southern and eastern Africa, these animals move in large groups that can number more than a million. Wildebeests are very defensive of their territory, and of their babies, called calves. At night, when the herd sleeps, a few animals remain awake, watching for intruders. If an animal tries to attack, the wildebeests work together to drive it away using sharp horns and hooves.

TRAP-JAW ANT

Meet some of the fastest jaws in the animal kingdom! Trap-jaw ants use their impressive-looking jaws to capture prey and to fight with other ants. Anything that brushes against special hairs on the insect's face triggers those massive mouthparts to slam shut. The ant's jaws aren't just speedy, either. They're strong enough to launch the insect into the air. One snap and the ant can propel itself more than 20 times its own body length—an impressive way to confuse and escape from predators.

CANADA LYNX

Living in a cold climate is *snow* problem for this cat! A Canada lynx's paws are extra furry and oversize, with toes that can spread wide. Lynx feet act like snowshoes, helping these cats stay on top of snow and get a good grip on icy surfaces. And that's not the only reason these animals are such good hunters. Their hind legs are longer than their front legs, which gives the Canada lynx a pouncing power that's bad news for their favorite prey, the snowshoe hare.

WOW!

BOBBIT WORM

The bobbit worm is a strong candidate for a fish's worst nightmare. Found in the waters of the Indo-Pacific, these lengthy worms burrow into the soft muck on the seafloor, leaving only their five antennae and large, open jaws visible. One soft brush against an antenna and—*SNAP!*—the worm's jaws slam shut around its prey, often with enough force to slice it in two. With a good grip on its meal, the worm then drags it down into the sand to eat.

WALRUS

Few animals will take on the mighty polar bear, but walruses are up for the challenge! Their tusks, which are overgrown teeth, can be up to three feet (1 m) long—plenty big enough to drive off the white bears that hunt walruses in their Arctic home. Walruses use their mighty tusks for other purposes, too. For instance, tusks help them haul their big bodies out of the water, and break holes in the ice so they can pop their heads up for a breath before returning to hunt for fish.

SNAPPING TURTLE

Snapping turtles, which look like they might have lived long ago with the dinosaurs, are one of the largest turtles in the world. They spend most of their lives buried in the muddy bottoms of lakes and rivers, coming up only once an hour or so to breathe. The turtle's tongue is bright red and looks a bit like a worm. It lures prey to its open mouth by wiggling its tongue ... then, snap! Its neck extends, its mouth closes, and the turtle earns its fierce name.

GREENLAND SHARK

This shark, a member of the sleeper shark family, may look like it's half asleep as it slowly moves through the deep, cold waters of the North Atlantic and Arctic Oceans. These fish use stealth and camouflage to sneak up on prey or scavenge for the remains of animals like moose and polar bears. While they won't win any awards for speed, Greenland sharks have one of the longest life spans of any animal on Earth. Most live to at least 200, and the oldest Greenland sharks are probably more than 500 years old!

KOALA

This little baby, called a joey, uses its claws to hang on to its mom's back for now, but when it grows up, it will use them to drive away predators. Despite their name, koalas aren't bears, but they can be surprisingly fierce and have bad tempers around humans. They tend to be nicer to their own kind—male koalas generally keep their claws tucked away when they fight with other males, choosing to holler at each other from the treetops instead.

INDEX

Boldface indicates illustrations.

A

Adélie penguins 70, **70**
African buffalo 46–47, **46–47**
African crested rats 90, **90**
African elephants 149, **149**
African giant swallowtails 166, **166**
African wild dogs 24–25, **24–25**
Alligators 106, **106**
American alligators 106, **106**
American badgers 112, **112**
Anacondas 20, **20**
Anglerfish 17, **17**
Anteaters 69, **69**, 181, **181**
Ants
    bullet ants 79, **79**
    driver ants 86, **86**
    fire ants 184, **184**
    trap-jaw ants 201, **201**
Appetites, deadly 68–69, **68–69**
Arctic foxes 146–147, **146–147**
Armadillos 140, **140**
Assassin bugs 62, **62**
Atlantic wolffish 16, **16**

B

Baboons 63, **63**
Badgers 54, **54,** 112, **112**

Barracuda 196, **196**
Barred owls 114, **114**
Bats 68, **68,** 170–171, **170–171**
Bearded dragons 148, **148**
Bears
    giant pandas 35, **35**
    grizzly bears **1,** 13, **13**
    polar bears 132, **132**
Beavers 83, **83**
Bees 28, **28,** 177, **177**
Beetles 92–93, **92–93,** 104, **104**
Bengal tigers 64–65, **64–65**
Big-horned sheep 138, **138**
Bird-dropping spiders 156, **156**
Birds
    Adélie penguins 70, **70**
    barred owls 114, **114**
    Canada geese 144, **144**
    cassowaries 14, **14**
    crowned eagles 199, **199**
    cuckoos 43, **43**
    Dalmatian pelicans 94, **94**
    fulmars 130, **130**
    golden eagles 142, **142**
    great blue herons 180, **180**
    great horned owls 169, **169**
    ground finches 86, **86**
    harpy eagles 32, **32**
    hoatzins 158, **158**
    hoopoes 105, **105**

    northern shrikes 101, **101**
    ostriches 188–189, **188–189**
    peregrine falcons **110–111,** 111
    pitohui 121, **121**
    red-tailed hawks 48, **48**
    turkey vultures 104, **104**
    vultures 104, **104,** 123, **123**
Bite force, most powerful 86–87, **86–87**
Black caimans 198, **198**
Black-footed cats 119, **119**
Black mambas 57, **57**
Black widow spiders **3,** 125, **125**
Blue glaucus sea slugs 151, **151**
Blue-ringed octopuses 82, **82**
Blue whales 68, **68**
Bobbit worms 203, **203**
Body parts, deadly 140–141, **140–141**
Bombardier beetles 92–93, **92–93**
Boomslangs **52–53**
Box jellyfish 73, **73**
Brazilian wandering spiders 131, **131**
Brown bats 68, **68**
Brown recluse spiders 72, **72**
Bruno's casque-headed frogs 53

Budgett's frogs 150, **150**
Buffalo 46–47, **46–47**
Bull sharks 87, **87**
Bullet ants 79, **79**
Bumblebees 28, **28**, 177, **177**
Butterflies **53**, 166, **166**

C

Caimans 198, **198**
Canada geese 144, **144**
Canada lynx 202, **202**
Cane toads 42, **42**
Cassowaries 14, **14**
Cat family
    Bengal tigers 64–65, **64–65**
    black-footed cats 119, **119**
    Canada lynx 202, **202**
    cheetahs 88, **88**
    cougars 137, **137**
    house cats 21, **21**
    jaguars 56, **56**
    jaguarundi 77, **77**
    leopards 84, **84**
    lions 128–129, **128–129**
    snow leopards 120, **120**
Cattle 37, **37**
Cheetahs 88, **88**
Chimpanzees 71, **71**

Claws
    American badgers 112, **112**
    cassowaries 14, **14**
    cheetahs 88, **88**
    coconut crabs 113, **113**
    fishers 162, **162**
    giant armadillos 140, **140**
    great horned owls 169, **169**
    grizzly bears 13
    harpy eagles 32, **32**
    honey badgers 54, **54**
    koalas 207, **207**
    mantis shrimp 116, **116–117**
    ostriches 188, **188–189**
    prairie dogs 107, **107**
    scorpions 157, **157**
    tamanduas 181, **181**
    water monitor lizards 191, **191**
Cobras 134–135, **134–135**
Coconut crabs 113, **113**
Cone snails 139, **139**
Coral snakes 176, **176**
Corroboree frogs 6, **6**
Cottonmouths 66, **66**
Cougars 137, **137**
Cows 37, **37**
Coyotes 38, **38**
Crabs 113, **113**, 179, **179**

Crocodiles, saltwater 51, **51**
Crowned eagles 199, **199**
Cuckoos 43, **43**
Cute but deadly 34–35, **34–35**
Cuttlefish 127, **127**

D

Daddy longlegs 122, **122**
Dalmatian pelicans 94, **94**
Deer 34, **34**, 141, **141**
Dholes 186, **186**
Dingoes 175, **175**
Dog family
    African wild dogs 24–25, **24–25**
    arctic foxes 146–147, **146–147**
    coyotes 38, **38**
    dholes 186, **186**
    dingoes 175, **175**
    gray wolves 9, **9**
Dogfish **53**
Dolphins 168, **168**
Dragonflies 152–153, **152–153**
Driver ants 86, **86**

E

Eagles
    crowned eagles 199, **199**
    golden eagles 142, **142**

INDEX

harpy eagles 32, **32**
Earwigs 123, **123**
Electric eels 100, **100**
Elephant seals **194–195**, 195
Elephants 149, **149**
European moles 29, **29**

F
Fakes 176–177, **176–177**
Falcons **110–111**, 111
Finches 86, **86**
Fire ants 184, **184**
Fish
    anglerfish 17, **17**
    Atlantic wolffish 16, **16**
    barracuda 196, **196**
    bull sharks 87, **87**
    deep sea 16–17, **16–17**
    dogfish **53**
    electric eels 100, **100**
    frilled sharks 55, **55**
    goblin sharks 16, **16**
    great white sharks 4–5, **4–5**
    Greenland sharks 206, **206**
    hagfish 12, **12**
    hammerhead sharks 143, **143**
    lampreys 187, **187**
    lionfish 108, **108**
    piranhas 133, **133**
    pufferfish 164–165, **164–165**

reef stonefish 124, **124**
sailfish 161, **161**
snakeheads 190, **190**
stingrays 22, **22**
thresher sharks 140, **140**
tiger sharks 96, **96**
Fishers 162, **162**
Flannel moth caterpillars 193, **193**
Foxes 146–147, **146–147**
Frilled sharks 55, **55**
Frogs
    Bruno's casque-headed frogs **53**
    Budgett's frogs 150, **150**
    corroboree frogs 6, **6**
    golden dart frogs 18–19, **18–19**
    wolverine frogs 49, **49**
Fulmars 130, **130**

G
Geese 144, **144**
Giant African land snails 50, **50**
Giant anteaters 69, **69**
Giant armadillos 140, **140**
Giant hornets 8, **8**
Giant pandas 35, **35**
Gila monsters 89, **89**
Giraffes 98–99, **98–99**

Goblin sharks 16, **16**
Golden dart frogs 18–19, **18–19**
Golden eagles 142, **142**
Gorillas 126, **126**
Grass moths 177, **177**
Gray wolves 9, **9**
Great blue herons 180, **180**
Great horned owls 169, **169**
Great white sharks 4–5, **4–5**
Greenland sharks 206, **206**
Grizzly bears **1**, 13, **13**
Gross defenses 104–105, **104–105**
Ground finches 86, **86**

H
Hagfish 12, **12**
Hammerhead sharks 143, **143**
Harpy eagles 32, **32**
Hedgehogs 33, **33**
Herons 180, **180**
Hippos **182–183**, 183
Hoatzins 158, **158**
Honey badgers 54, **54**
Hoopoes 105, **105**
Horned lizards 85, **85**
Hornet moths 172, **172**
Hornets 8, **8**
Horses 173, **173**
House cats 21, **21**

Humboldt squid 197, **197**
Hyenas 118, **118**

I

Iberian ribbed newts 97, **97**
Iguanas 26, **26**
Inland taipans 103, **103**
Insects
  African giant swallowtails
    166, **166**
  assassin bugs 62, **62**
  bombardier beetles 92–93,
    92–93
  bullet ants 79, **79**
  bumblebees 28, **28**, 177, **177**
  dragonflies 152–153, **152–153**
  driver ants 86, **86**
  earwigs 123, **123**
  fire ants 184, **184**
  flannel moth caterpillars
    193, **193**
  giant hornets 8, **8**
  grass moths 177, **177**
  hornet moths 172, **172**
  mosquitoes 145, **145**
  potato beetles 104, **104**
  praying mantises 45, **45**
  robber flies 177, **177**
  stinkbugs 158, **158**

  tarantula hawks 67, **67**
  tiger moths 177, **177**
  trap-jaw ants 201, **201**
  yellow jackets 160, **160**

J

Jaguars 56, **56**
Jaguarundi 77, **77**
Japanese spider crabs 179, **179**
Jellyfish 73, **73**

K

Kangaroos 136, **136**
Killer whales (orcas) 80–81,
  80–81
King snakes 176, **176**
Koalas 207, **207**
Komodo dragons **2,** 40–41,
  40–41

L

Lampreys 187, **187**
Lanceheads 44, **44**
Leopard seals 174, **174**
Leopards 84, **84**
Lionfish 108, **108**
Lions 128–129, **128–129**

Lizards
  bearded dragons 148, **148**
  Gila monsters 89, **89**
  horned lizards 85, **85**
  iguanas 26, **26**
  Komodo dragons **2,** 40–41,
    40–41
  water monitors 191, **191**
Lorises 74–75, **74–75**
Lynx 202, **202**

M

Mantis shrimp 116–117, **116–117**
Mantises 45, **45**
Meerkats 30–31, **30–31**
Millipedes 61, **61**
Moles 29, **29**
Monarch butterflies **53**
Mongooses 115, **115**
Moose 163, **163**
Mosquitoes 145, **145**
Moths
  flannel moth caterpillars
    193, **193**
  grass moths or tiger moths?
    177, **177**
  hornet moths 172, **172**
Musk deer 141, **141**
Myths busted 122–123, **122–123**

INDEX

N

Newts 97, **97**
North American rattlesnakes 76, **76**
Northern shrikes 101, **101**

O

Octopuses 82, **82**
Orcas 80–81, **80–81**
Ostriches 188–189, **188–189**
Otters 91, **91**
Owls 114, **114**, 169, **169**

P

Palythoa 27, **27**
Pandas, giant 35, **35**
Peccaries 178, **178**
Pelicans 94, **94**
Penguins 70, **70**
Peregrine falcons **110–111**, 111
Piranhas 133, **133**
Pit vipers 44, **44**, 66, **66**
Pitohui 121, **121**
Platypuses 39, **39**
Poisonous or venomous? 52–53, **52–53**
Polar bears 132, **132**
Poop 104, 156
Porcupines 7, **7**

Portuguese man-of-wars 58–59, **58–59**
Potato beetles 104, **104**
Prairie dogs 107, **107**
Praying mantises 45, **45**
Pufferfish 164–165, **164–165**
Pythons 192, **192**

R

Raccoons 167, **167**
Rats 90, **90**
Rattlesnakes 76, **76**
Red-tailed hawks 48, **48**
Reef stonefish 124, **124**
Rhabdophis **53**
Rhinoceroses 109, **109**
Robber flies 177, **177**

S

Sailfish 161, **161**
Saltwater crocodiles 51, **51**
Scorpions 157, **157**
Sea cucumbers 36, **36**
Sea lions 95, **95**
Sea otters 91, **91**
Sea slugs 151, **151**
Sea urchins 155, **155**
Seals 174, **174**, **194–195**, 195
Sharks
    bull sharks 87, **87**

frilled sharks 55, **55**
goblin sharks 16, **16**
great white sharks 4–5, **4–5**
Greenland sharks 206, **206**
hammerhead sharks 143, **143**
thresher sharks 140, **140**
tiger sharks 96, **96**
Sheep 138, **138**
Shocking pink dragon millipedes 61, **61**
Shrikes 101, **101**
Shrimp 116–117, **116–117**
Skunks 159, **159**
Slow lorises 74–75, **74–75**
Smells, toxic 158–159, **158–159**
Snails 50, **50**, 139, **139**
Snakeheads 190, **190**
Snakes
    anacondas 20, **20**
    black mambas 57, **57**
    boomslangs **52–53**
    cottonmouths 66, **66**
    inland taipans 103, **103**
    king snake or coral snake? 176, **176**
    lanceheads 44, **44**
    North American rattlesnakes 76, **76**
    pythons 192, **192**
    Rhabdophis **53**

spitting cobras 134–135, **134–135**
Snapping turtles 205, **205**
Snow leopards 120, **120**
Solenodons 23, **23**
Sperm whales 78, **78**
Spider crabs 179, **179**
Spiders
  bird-dropping spiders 156, **156**
  black widows **3,** 125, **125**
  Brazilian wandering spiders 131, **131**
  brown recluses 72, **72**
  daddy longlegs 122, **122**
  tarantulas 10–11, **10–11**
Spitting cobras 134–135, **134–135**
Squid 197, **197**
Stingrays 22, **22**
Stinkbugs 158, **158**
Stonefish 124, **124**

T
Tamanduas 181, **181**
Tarantula hawks 67, **67**
Tarantulas 10–11, **10–11**
Tasmanian devils 15, **15**
Teeth
  Atlantic wolffish 16, **16**

baboons 63, **63**
barracuda 196, **196**
beavers 83, **83**
dolphins 168, **168**
frilled sharks 55, **55**
great white sharks 4, **4,** 5
lampreys 187, **187**
musk deer 141, **141**
orcas 80
piranhas 133
pufferfish 164
walruses 204, **204**
warthogs 154, **154**
see also Bite force, most powerful
Textile cone snails 139, **139**
Thresher sharks 140, **140**
Tiger moths 177, **177**
Tiger quolls 34, **34**
Tiger sharks 96, **96**
Tigers 64–65, **64–65**
Toads 42, **42**
Trap-jaw ants 201, **201**
Turkey vultures 104, **104**
Turtles 205, **205**

V
Vampire bats 170–171, **170–171**

Venomous or poisonous? 52–53, **52–53**
Vomit 104, 130, **130,** 157
Vultures 104, **104,** 123, **123**

W
Walruses 204, **204**
Warthogs 154, **154**
Wasps 67, **67,** 160, **160**
Water monitor lizards 191, **191**
Whales 68, **68,** 78, **78**
White-tailed deer 34, **34**
Wild boars 102, **102**
Wildebeests 200, **200**
Wolverine frogs 49, **49**
Wolverines 185, **185**
Wolves 9, **9**
Worms 203, **203**

Y
Yellow jackets 160, **160**

Z
Zebras 60, **60**

PHOTO CREDITS

Front Cover: (tiger), Espen Bergersen/Nature Picture Library; (snake), kuritafsheen/AD; (scorpion), Jason Bazzano/AL; (shark), Chris & Monique Fallows/Nature Picture Library; **Spine:** Espen Bergersen/Nature Picture Library; **Back Cover:** (falcon), Harry Collins/AD; (hippo), Wlad74/SS; **Interior:** 1, Joel Sartore/National Geographic Image Collection; 2, Uryadnikov Sergey/AD; 3, Jacob Hamblin/SS; 4-5, elsahoffmann/AD; 6, Jean-Paul Ferrero/Auscape International Pty Ltd/AL; 7, teekayu/SS; 8, mohsin/AD; 9, PHOTO 24/GI; 10-11, K.D. Leperi/AL; 12, Mark Conlin/AL; 13, Cavan Images/AD; 14, mujiri/SS; 15, AndriiSlonchak/GI; 16 (UP), Poelzer Wolfgang/AL; 16 (LO), Kelvin Aitken/VWPics/AL; 17, Solvin Zankl/Nature Picture Library; 18-19, Thorsten Spoerlein/AD; 20, Jason Edwards/AL; 21, FurryFritz/AD; 22, Stephen Frink/Digital Vision Life Underwater; 23, Joel Sartore/Photo Ark/National Geographic Image Collection; 24-25, Paul Souders/GI; 26, Jillian Cain/AD; 27, Paul Starosta/GI; 28, Ian Grainger/SS; 29, Avalon/Universal Images Group/GI; 30-31, Gunter/AD; 32, MarcusVDT/SS; 33, praisaeng/AD; 34 (UP), Craig Dingle/SS; 34 (LO), KenCanning/GI; 34 (LO RT), Eric Lowenbach/GI; 35, clkraus/SS; 36, Ethan Daniels/SS; 37, Pierluigi.Palazzi/SS; 38, Nina/AD; 39, Doug Gimesy/Nature Picture Library; 40-41, Nicolas Cegalerba/Hemis.fr/AL; 42, Chris Ison/SS; 43, J.C.Salvadores/AD; 44, David/AD; 45, lessysebastian/AD; 46-47, NiStar PS/GI; 48, Amy Surowiec/GI; 49, Paul Starosta/GI; 50, FLPA/SS; 51, Zoe Ezzy/SS; 52 (LE), Valeriy Kirsanov/AD; 52 (RT), Leonardo/AD; 53 (UP LE), Duncan Noakes/AD; 53 (UP RT), Joern_k/SS; 53 (LO LE), photoncatcher36/AD; 53 (LO RT), David Anderson/Dreamstime; 54, Braam Collins/SS; 55, Awashima Marine Park/SS; 56, Nick Garbutt/Nature Picture Library; 57, mgkuijpers/AD; 58-59, Charlotte/AD; 60, Karlos Lomsky/AD; 61, freeman98589/AD; 62, Husni Che Ngah/Minden Pictures; 63, ZSSD/Minden Pictures; 64-65, Milan/AD; 66, Riverwalker/AD; 67, Rick & Nora Bowers/AL; 68 (UP), Joe McDonald/GI; 68 (LO), Darin Sakdatorn/AD; 69, esdeem/SS; 70, WorldFoto/AD; 71, ondrejprosicky/AD; 72, Phil Degginger/AL; 73, Gary Bell/Oceanwide/Minden Pictures; 74-75, Thomas Marent/Minden Pictures; 76, randimal/GI; 77, Michal Sloviak/SS; 78, Reinhard Dirscherl/GI; 79, Anton Sorokin/AL; 80-81, slowmotiongli/AD; 82, the Ocean Agency/AD; 83, Troy Harrison/GI; 84, Thilanka Perera/GI; 85, Milan Zygmunt/SS; 86 (UP), Pavel Krasensky/SS; 86 (LO), Pete Oxford/Nature Picture Library; 87, Terry Moore/Stocktrek Images/AL; 88, Stu Porter/SS; 89, vaclav/AD; 90, Sara Weinstein; 91, Jody J. Overstreet/AD; 92-93, Satoshi Kuribayashi/Minden Pictures; 94, Iliuta/AD; 95, Joost van Uffelen/SS; 96, Rodrigo Friscione/AD; 97, Viter8/Dreamstime; 98-99, Olma/AD; 100, Kseniia Mnasina/SS; 101, fsanchex/AD; 102, Natureimmortal/AD; 103, Ken Griffiths/AD; 104 (UP), giedriius/AD; 104 (LO), Andrzej Wilusz/SS; 105, Grzegorz Lesniewski/Minden Pictures; 106, hakoar/AD; 107, Petr/AD; 108, Pierluigi Leggeri/AD; 109, Volodymy Burdiak/AD; 110-111, Keith K/SS; 112, Tom Murphy/National Geographic Image Collection; 113, Stephen Belcher/Minden Pictures; 114, Scott Suriano/GI; 115, Dave Hamman/Gallo Images/GI; 116-117, Paul Starosta/GI; 118, Abdelrahman/AD; 119, Pardofelis Photography/AD; 120, Steve Winter/National Geographic Image Collection; 121, Wirestock, Inc./AL; 122, Rainer Fuhrmann/AD; 123 (UP), Maryke/AD; 123 (LO), Eric Isselee/SS; 124, Kristina Vackova/SS; 125, Mark Kostich/GI; 126, Christophe Courteau/Nature Picture Library; 127, Andrea Izzotti/AD; 128-129, Alexandre Fiocre/GI; 130, Jouan Rius/Nature Picture Library; 131, tacio philip/AD; 132, Andrew Stewart/Specialiststock/Splashdown/SS; 133, Kokhanchikov/SS; 134-135, Digital Vision/GI; 136, Stefano Unterthiner/National Geographic Image Collection; 137, Sumio Harada/Minden Pictures; 138, Nick Trehearne/All Canada Photos/AL; 139, Laura Dts/SS; 140 (UP), Kevin Schafer/GI; 140 (LO), Norbert Probst/imageBROKER/SS; 141, TashaBubo/SS; 142, Karel Bartik/SS; 143, frantisekhojdysz/SS; 144, Chefmd/GI; 145, Dmitrijs Bindemanis/SS; 146-147, Paul/AD; 148, Ashley Whitworth/AD; 149, Manoj Shah/GI; 150, Milan Zygmunt/SS; 151, LeticiaLara/AD; 152-153, Santiago mc/GI; 154, Mike/AD; 155, Brent Durand/GI; 156, Alen Thien/SS; 157, Iamyai/AD; 158 (UP), YuanGeng/AD; 158 (LO), Tomas Drahos/SS; 159, Stan Tekiela/AD; 160, Sean McVey/SS; 161, Michael Valos/AD; 162, slowmotiongli/AD; 163, Dieter Hopf/GI; 164-165, David Fleetham/AL; 166, Darrell Gulin/Danita Delimont/AL; 167, jadimages/SS; 168, Jeff Mondragon/AL; 169, Ondrej Chvatal/SS; 170-171, Photoshot/Avalon.red/AL; 172, Westend61/GI; 173, Ruth Ann Johnston/GI; 174, Paul Nicklen/National Geographic Image Collection; 175, Matt Cornish/SS; 176 (UP), ondreicka/AD; 176 (LO), Radiant Reptilia/AD; 177 (UP LE), Den/AD; 177 (UP RT), blackdiamond67/AD; 177 (LO LE), Maier, R./Juniors Bildarchiv GmbH/AL; 177 (LO RT), Tim's insects/AD; 178, Mark Newman/GI; 179, Ken Usami/GI; 180, mzphoto11/AD; 181, Luciano Candisani/Minden Pictures; 182-183, Sren Pedersen/EyeEm/GI; 184, sarawuth123/AD; 185, Richard Seeley/National Geographic Image Collection; 186, esp2k/AD; 187, GDM photo and video/AD; 188-189, bruna-nature/SS; 190, Zhang Zhiwei/Zoonar/AL; 191, Traiyot Janvanishsakul/SS; 192, Matthijs Kuijpers/AL; 193, George Grall/AL; 194-195, Jeremy Richards/AD; 196, Rainervon Brandis/GI; 197, Franco Banfi/Nature Picture Library; 198, vaclav/AD; 199, Joel Sartore/National Geographic Image Collection; 200, Johan Swanepoel/SS; 201, AEyZRiO/AD; 202, Sebastian Kennerknecht/Minden Pictures; 203, anemone/AD; 204, Mikhail Cheremkin/AD; 205, Yoaspermadi/SS; 206, Franco Banfi/Nature Picture Library; 207, Ben Twist/AD

For Jeff: the sibling without equal —J.S.

Since 1888, the National Geographic Society has funded more than 14,000 research, conservation, education, and storytelling projects around the world. National Geographic Partners distributes a portion of the funds it receives from your purchase to National Geographic Society to support programs including the conservation of animals and their habitats. To learn more, visit natgeo.com/info.

For more information, visit nationalgeographic.com, call 1-877-873-6846, or write to the following address:

National Geographic Partners, LLC
1145 17th Street NW
Washington, DC 20036-4688 U.S.A.

For librarians and teachers: nationalgeographic.com/books/librarians-and-educators

More for kids from National Geographic: natgeokids.com

National Geographic Kids magazine inspires children to explore their world with fun yet educational articles on animals, science, nature, and more. Using fresh storytelling and amazing photography, *Nat Geo Kids* shows kids ages 6 to 14 the fascinating truth about the world—and why they should care. **natgeo.com/subscribe**

For rights or permissions inquiries, please contact National Geographic Books Subsidiary Rights: bookrights@natgeo.com

Designed by Amanda Larsen, Gustavo Tello, and Mary Wages

Library of Congress Cataloging-in-Publication Data

Names: National Geographic Society (U.S.)
Title: Deadliest animals on the planet / National Geographic Kids.
Description: Washington, D.C. : National Geographic Kids, 2023. I Includes index. I Audience: Ages 8-12 I Audience: Grades 4-6
Identifiers: LCCN 2021043380 I ISBN 9781426373183 (paperback) I ISBN 9781426374326 (library binding)
Subjects: LCSH: Dangerous animals--Juvenile literature.
Classification: LCC QL100 .D434 2023 I DDC 591.6/5--dc23
LC record available at https://lccn.loc.gov/2021043380

The publisher would like to thank Jen Szymanski, author and researcher; Grace Hill Smith, project manager; Avery Naughton, project editor; Colin Wheeler, photo editor; Jennifer Geddes, fact-checker; Alix Inchausti, senior production editor, and David Marvin and Lauren Sciortino, associate designers.

Printed in China
23/PPS/1

LOOK OUT!

This book might GRAB YOU!

NATIONAL GEOGRAPHIC KiDS

ULTIMATE PREDATOR-PEDIA

THE MOST COMPLETE PREDATOR REFERENCE EVER

CHRISTINA WILSDON

Sink your teeth into COOL FACTS and PHOTOS